Cambridge Elements ≡

Elements in Translation and Interpreting
edited by
Kirsten Malmkjær
University of Leicester

TOWARDS GAME TRANSLATION USER RESEARCH

Mikołaj Deckert
University of Lodz

Krzysztof W. Hejduk
University of Lodz

Miguel Á. Bernal-Merino
Localisation Consultant

CAMBRIDGE
UNIVERSITY PRESS

Shaftesbury Road, Cambridge CB2 8EA, United Kingdom

One Liberty Plaza, 20th Floor, New York, NY 10006, USA

477 Williamstown Road, Port Melbourne, VIC 3207, Australia

314–321, 3rd Floor, Plot 3, Splendor Forum, Jasola District Centre,
New Delhi – 110025, India

103 Penang Road, #05–06/07, Visioncrest Commercial, Singapore 238467

Cambridge University Press is part of Cambridge University Press & Assessment,
a department of the University of Cambridge.

We share the University's mission to contribute to society through the pursuit of
education, learning and research at the highest international levels of excellence.

www.cambridge.org
Information on this title: www.cambridge.org/9781009509800

DOI: 10.1017/9781009385824

When citing this work, please include a reference to the DOI 10.1017/9781009385824

First published 2024

A catalogue record for this publication is available from the British Library.

ISBN 978-1-009-50980-0 Hardback
ISBN 978-1-009-38581-7 Paperback
ISSN 2633-6480 (online)
ISSN 2633-6472 (print)

Towards Game Translation User Research

Elements in Translation and Interpreting

DOI: 10.1017/9781009385824
First published online: May 2024

Mikołaj Deckert
University of Lodz

Krzysztof W. Hejduk
University of Lodz

Miguel Á. Bernal-Merino
Localisation Consultant

Author for correspondence: Mikołaj Deckert, mikolaj.deckert@uni.lodz.pl

Abstract: This Element takes the initiative to highlight the nascent state of audiovisual translation research centring on users of video games. It proposes ways of advancing the research by integrating numerous related perspectives from relevant fields to guide studies in translated game reception into further fruition. The Element offers an accessible overview of possible relationships between translation and its experiencers, showcasing ways to design game reception studies. Examples, methods, tools, and practical concerns are discussed to ultimately develop a blueprint for game translation user research which aims to consolidate scientific user-centric inquiry into video game translation. To that end, the blueprint captures the three-pronged interplay between the parameters of localisation-reception research in facets of user experience, facets of translated games, and facets of game users.

Keywords: game users, interlingual translation, localisation, user experience, player experience

ISBNs: 9781009509800 (HB), 9781009385817 (PB), 9781009385824 (OC)
ISSNs: 2633-6480 (online), 2633-6472 (print)

Contents

1 What Has Been Done So Far – An Overview

The gaming industry as well as scholarly circles are increasingly interested in studying user experience [UX] and game playability. Probing aspects of players' reception of video games naturally synergises with developing good practices not only in design, but also in game localisation and game accessibility research. Despite this, Audiovisual Translation [AVT] and Media Accessibility [MA] research centring on individuals engaging with games (i.e. players, but also viewers of gameplay) is yet underdeveloped and fragmented. Such an observation is all the more striking considering that the global success of the industry largely rests on practices of globalisation, internationalisation, localisation, and translation [GILT] (cf. O'Hagan 2005). For at least a decade now, the games industry has been putting 'more focus [...] on the players and how to design around an intensely pleasurable player experience' (Nacke & Lindley 2009: 2). Although it remains in a largely nascent state, an interest in the study of *game localisation* from a user-based perspective can also be observed. This Element thus opens with a review of existing research that adopted a player perspective on video games [VGs] and translation (see: Section 1.1). A survey of publications makes it possible to systematise what has been done and identify multiple areas where user-centric research remains to be conducted – the 'how' of which is explored further on (cf. Sections 2–4).

1.1 User-Centric Research in Video Game Translation

Let us introduce research that we can call *user-centric* (or perhaps *users-centric*, to highlight the plurality of VG interactants). That work can be viewed as part of what Carme Mangiron (2017: 85) calls 'participant-oriented' research which covers a wider range of agents, including those who represent the perspective of production (translators, developers, localisation vendors, and producers). While an overview of the type attempted here can hardly be exhaustive, we aspire to provide the reader with a well-informed insight into the scale and range of the VG translation work to date that adopts the vantage point of users. Let us begin this overview by pointing out that the observation voiced by Minako O'Hagan (2009: 212–213) some fifteen years ago appears to remain valid today: 'While many game developments incorporate a form of player input through beta testing, focus group sessions etc to ensure that the game has the intended impact on the user, player reaction is usually not part of formal testing for localised games above and beyond the aspects captured by functional and linguistic testing.'

This remark contextualises the study she reports, done with an English native speaker playing a localised English version of the originally Japanese game *Ico* (Japan Studio & Team Ico 2001). Several types of data were collected in the experiment such as the play trajectory, recording of the participant's hand movements, as well as the verbal input the participant produced during gameplay. Additionally, pauses in playing were used to elicit feedback through a template-based game log. This was supplemented with a retrospective interview. The experiment lasted for a total of 11.5 hours spanning five days. The analysis of what O'Hagan (2009) terms 'the Player [sic] experience data' makes it possible for her to isolate several areas: freedom of play, language, back story, user interface [UI], graphics, AI design, and force-feedback (controller vibration). She finds, for example, that the participant felt frustrated by the game's semi-controlled camera angles, a feature associated with Japanese games more than with Western games, which are less constraining in that respect.

The study does not strive to offer a systematically contrastive perspective on how different versions of a game are experienced. It is in later studies where Minako O'Hagan (2016) as well as Minako O'Hagan and Marian Flanagan (2018) adopt this type of perspective, collecting data from players who engaged with an English original as well as two translated versions of the game, a German and a Japanese one (O'Hagan 2016), and German, Japanese as well as Irish versions (O'Hagan & Flanagan 2018), which makes it possible to isolate localisation as a parameter that can influence reception. In the 2009 paper the author nonetheless comes up with such contrastive insights drawing on feedback from players who engaged with the Japanese version, as relayed by the production team, among others. Specifically, a separate extensive category is termed 'cultural differences in the emotional appeal of a localised game' (O'Hagan 2009: 226). An interesting point brought up here is that there are observable differences in how the participant interacted with and reasoned about one of the game characters compared to Japanese players. At the same time, O'Hagan (2009: 229) points out that a most important takeaway is that the game under scrutiny deployed non-verbal means to hold emotional appeal universally across cultures.

A different approach was chosen by Alberto Fernández-Costales (2016) who conducted a study involving 94 participants. He utilised the Game Users Translation Survey (GUTSY) with 20 items that were replied to on a 1–4 Likert-type scale. His guiding hypothesis was that players prefer a foreignising approach in the sense that they would opt for the translated version to retain 'the "look and feel" of the original product and also the cultural references and other elements from the source text' (Fernández-Costales 2016: 185). The second underlying question that he aimed to answer concerned the occurrence of code-switching understood as turning to Spanish instead of English when playing or interacting with a game's *para-texts*. The results are interesting in a number of respects.

For example, participants tended to agree that 'A video game has been properly translated when you do not feel it has been designed in a different language' but were less convinced that'Playing video games in Spanish improves the game experience'. What is more, respondents tended to agree that they liked VGs to keep the source cultural references unaltered and 'Elements such as names, locations, equipment, etc., should never be translated'. As Fernández-Costales (2016: 192) observes, some of these patterns are to some extent contradictory since a preference for a source-oriented approach would entail that participants could expect to be able to recognise that the original product was created in a different language. Still, he ascribes this to the *social desirability bias*, thus offering a valuable methodological insight into the use of survey data (cf. Section 2 on *facets of user experience*).

Further on, as participants mostly agreed they visited the websites of the games they like, they also mostly chose not to concur that they always visited the official websites of games in their native language. Some other thought-provoking results are that most participants do not see the lack of a Spanish version of a game as something that would prevent them from buying the game. Linked to that, the participant pool displays a tendency to disagree that all VGs should be translated into Spanish or, even more visibly, that games should be adapted into minority languages or co-official languages (cf. Section 3 on *facets of translated games*). Another notable finding is that a clear preponderance of participants liked playing VGs in English and while, as Fernández-Costales (2016: 195) rightly notes, this does not necessarily imply a preference for games in English over games in one's mother tongue, it could be highlighting the status of English which could be changing user habits and gaming preferences.

Relevantly for the current Element, while Fernández-Costales' study comes from the recognition that there is little research into user perceptions and preferences when it comes to translation of multimedia interactive software (Fernández-Costales 2016: 184; cf. O'Hagan 2009) and he stresses that 'users need to be taken into account in Translation Studies' (Fernández-Costales 2016: 198), he also notes that his research 'does not support an "enthronement" of users' perceptions so that they have a major influence on the whole translation process or in the development of theoretical models and frameworks, but rather that investigation in Translation Studies include final users so they are not ignored' (Fernández-Costales 2016: 198). While this disclaimer relevantly discerns the translation process and the theoretical dimension of translation studies, the distinction does not seem sufficient to explain where exactly the influence of users should cease.

In a similar methodological vein, Ugo Ellefsen and Miguel Á. Bernal-Merino (2018) report their survey-based study whose aim was to give an account of the linguistic preferences of Francophone players from Belgium, France, Canada, and Switzerland. Input from 726 gamers was received, which made it possible to identify many patterns, some of which link directly back to the data collected by Fernández-Costales (2016). For instance, French-speaking players tend to prefer a foreignising approach with respect to the source text's names, places, and cultural references. The source-oriented approach was then consistently manifested when it comes to whether 'content deemed offensive should always be censored' via localisation where participants disagreed in a rather pronounced way (Ellefsen & Bernal-Merino 2018: 38).

Another concrete result is that there was a preference among players for subtitling over dubbing. As for the study's working hypothesis that there would be some mismatch in linguistic preferences between players from multilingual locales (Belgium, Canada, Switzerland), it turned out to be true for the Canadian sub-pool. Overall, Ellefsen and Bernal-Merino (2018: 41) construe the French-speaking community as a '*fandom*' in that it is 'a highly critical and mobilised consumer base' whose influence on the industry should be factored in as content is produced. They highlight a point that we will return to in Section 3 on *facets of translated games* and Section 4 on *facets of game users*, which is that while language could be seen as a common denominator of receptor groups viewed as 'monolithic cultural constructs when it comes to localised products', there are in fact 'more factors that shape the attitudes of a community towards a given cultural production than the use of a common language within set geographical borders'.

Drawing on their results as well as on one of the authors' unpublished essays (Ellefsen 2015) and an MA project (Roh 2011), Ellefsen and Bernal-Merino (2018: 42–43) make three recommendations for the VG industry. The first one, which is to *engage*, is a call for inviting the community to get involved in the development of best practices and creating feedback loops to benefit VG localisation. Second, localisation practices need to be *standardised*, similarly to how film subtitles are produced following certain guidelines. Finally, the authors recommend language customisation – or *personalisation* – that is offering players more choice regarding 'how they want to experience the narrative through dubbing, subtitling, partial translation or non-translation', which they see as a logical extension of customisation in other dimensions of games (Ellefsen & Bernal-Merino 2018: 43).

More recent studies include those by Dominik Kudła (2021) who elicited and analysed input from 395 Polish players, and Masood Khoshsaligheh and Saeed Ameri (2020) who were able to gather and examine data from a pool of 750 Iranian players. Likewise, in their two-pronged investigation, Mohammed Al-Batineh and Razan Alawneh (2022) combined a product-oriented perspective – analysing 142 localised games released within a span of over 15 years – and a reception perspective, with data on localisation preferences from 613 Arab gamers, while Zhiwei Wu and Zhuojia Chen (2020) embedded some highly implemental insights from game users in China in the context of game-localisation practices for Southeast Asia markets.

Another novel contribution comes with the work by Katayoon Afzali and Mahboobeh Zahiri (2022), representing a netnographic approach. In line with Robert V. Kozinets (2010), the authors define netnography as 'participant-observational research using computer-mediated communications as a source of data collection, and it aims to reach an ethnographic understanding and description of a cultural or communal phenomenon' (Afzali & Zahiri 2022: 77). The adjective 'ethnographic' is generally taken to denote approaches concerned with social behaviour across dimensions like race, nationality, religion, culture, and age (Afzali & Zahiri 2022: 88). The procedure comprised a number of steps, like creating a player account for the researcher, getting acquainted with gamer discourse and with the relevant games. In the course of 18 months 5000 comments were collected referring to a total of 8 games, using WhatsApp and game platforms to elicit data through communal interaction and interviews (cf. Kozinets 2010). Following Miguel Bernal-Merino's categorisation of in-game text, the authors singled out thematic categories of gamer input, centred on menus, game installer applications, system messages, dubbed and subtitled dialogues, narrations and game manuals. The results shed light on selected translation-related player preferences. For instance, only 5 per cent of players chose to play officially translated versions of games, compared to 15 per cent who opted for rom-hacked versions and as much as 80 per cent preferring untranslated versions. Another observation is that players tended to identify register mismatches with subtitles using more formal language than the original.

Other inquiries into game translation curiously include a relatively large pool of recent master theses (some of which remain unpublished) that rely on surveys, including those by:

- Quentin Faure (2020) – contrasted the opinions of users of French and Italian localisations, especially in terms of the differing guidelines on adapting proper names in the two locales;
- Francine Geurts (2015) – collected data from the Dutch locale in various user profiles, notably also non-gamers, finding that low-quality localisations limit game consumption there;
- Krzysztof W. Hejduk (2022) – used eyetracking and questionnaires with the help of Polish participants to explore the reception and potential localisability of *on-screen language*;

- Marion Hernandez (2017) – gathered assessments of localisation from francophone users, notably acknowledging the lack of scholarly focus on the reception of game translation;
- Julie Pigeon (2021) – surveyed various agents of the translational pipeline, including Canadian French end-users, to establish guidelines for good practice for translators.

Coming back to an experimental approach, as introduced with the case of work by Minako O'Hagan (2009), a study that is clearly trail-blazing in many respects is the one conducted by Carme Mangiron (2016). Drawing on her earlier research (Mangiron 2013), and motivated by the lack of standardisation in VG subtitling, she examined VG subtitling in terms of accessibility for deaf and hard-of-hearing receptors. Using eyetracker and questionnaire data from 25 participants she aimed to gain a better understanding of reception across the following parameters: subtitle presentation, subtitle alignment, reading speed, number of lines (2 vs. 3), character identification, and sound effects. Notably, the participant pool included hearing and deaf individuals. While exploratory in nature, as the author herself points out, the study offers a range of useful findings. Questionnaire data pointed to different preferences in subtitle presentation (including font parameters and different text boxes or lack thereof), which indicates that players would be best served by being able to choose their preferred game settings as a way to afford 'a more personalised and immersive gameplay experience' (Mangiron 2016: 16).

On the other hand, both hearing and hearing-impaired players preferred shorter two-line subtitles to longer one-line subtitles, and they mostly opted for their subtitles to be centred. At the same time, preferences were more varied between the two groups regarding whether subtitles are presented optimally in a box, a speech bubble, or without these, as well as how to identify characters (e.g. using an avatar, a name tag, or colour marking). Supplementing the questionnaire data with eyetracking evidence gathered in the experiment makes the account fuller and opens a number of possibilities for further research. For instance, the results show that two-line subtitles could be bringing an advantage in reading speed. This is notable because questionnaire data pointed in the same direction while, as Mangiron (2016: 15) observes, the common game subtitling practice is to deploy text in the form of a single line. She also found a difference in how successful two ways of conveying sound effects were, an onomatopoeic pop-up star-shaped box being visually registered much better than a blue text box displayed in the upper right-hand region of the screen. Another interesting result is that participants mostly did not allocate their visual attention to avatars.

The game utilised in the experiment by Carme Mangiron (2016), *Casa Encantada*, was developed by students at the Universitat Autònoma de Barcelona as their final project – which Mangiron (2016) sees as an issue to consider, mentioning that collaboration with industry developers is a productive way forward. Dominik Kudła (2020), in contrast, conducted an eyetracking study using a commercial game: *Shadow of the Tomb Raider* (Eidos-Montréal 2018). In this pioneering study, the fragment of the game included both cutscenes, which the players were instructed to watch, as well as gameplay where the participants controlled the playable character. Completing the portion of the game could take from ca. 4 minutes up to ca. 15 minutes. Kudła analysed reception data – gathered with an eyetracker and a questionnaire – from 39 participants who played 1 of 3 language versions of the game: a version which was fully localised into Polish, one that was localised partially, or the original English version. Subtitle settings were analogous for the three variants, with different speakers (altogether 11) in the game being colour-coded.

Kudła's study (2020) provides ample data across several dimensions of reception, demonstrating not only that eyetracking and questionnaires can provide valuable player experience information, but also that these two methods can be combined productively in a complementary fashion. One of the general findings of that study is that no significant differences were identified across the three versions of the game when it comes to visual processing. The participants' translation experience had no traceable impact either. The results partially confirmed the hypothesis that users would allocate more visual attentional resources – understood (cf. *operationalisation*, Section 2) as the eyetracking measures of glances count, dwell time, and average-fixation duration – to subtitles in cutscenes compared to subtitles during the players' active participation. No conclusive evidence was found to indicate that users who identify shortcomings in subtitles also distribute their visual attention differently, but there is some confirmatory evidence that formal training and translation experience increase one's likelihood of identifying such problems. Some of the other findings are that participants' amount of prior gaming experience is linked to average game fragment completion time. What is more, drawing on the differentiation proposed by Bartle (1996), Kudła (2020: 295) was able to isolate two playing strategies adopted by his participants. One group was more task-oriented while the other group played in a more exploratory manner. Notably, as the results indicate, the strategy was not shaped by the participants' translation or gaming experience, or the language version of the game.

Even more recently, experimental results were reported by Mikołaj Deckert and Krzysztof W. Hejduk (2022b, 2024). Similarly to Kudła (2020), they used as experimental stimuli an existing game: *Distraint: Deluxe Edition* (Makkonen 2015/2017), upon receiving the permission from the independent game developer Jesse Makkonen to conduct the research. Data sets from 201 participants completing a *ca.* 15-minute portion of the game were analysed across two conditions. The independent variable was spelling errors in the game's interlingual subtitles – twenty-five errors were inserted into the subtitles in the experimental condition while the control condition contained none. Deckert & Hejduk (2022b) examined reception data on three dimensions of player experience – cognitive load, comprehension, and enjoyment – as well as on the players' perception of the subtitles, their perception of the subtitler and their typo-identification success rate. The data showed that cognitive load, enjoyment, and comprehension were not significantly different because of the presence of typos. Similarly, the perceived profile of the subtitler (amateur vs. professional vs. hard to tell) was not traceably shaped by the experimental manipulation. At the same time, the translation with spelling errors was on average evaluated as inferior, and the author of that translation was seen as less diligent – but not as less experienced.

When it comes to spotting typos, a little less than 20 per cent of participants in the experimental condition mentioned typos when asked about anything they noticed about the subtitles. When explicitly asked about the possible presence of spelling deficiencies in the translated game they had played, players in the control condition were on average less likely to answer affirmatively. What is still remarkable, though, is that some players who played the version without typos reported registering some. Perhaps more intriguingly, over 37 per cent of players in the experimental condition conversely stated they saw no typos. As a follow-up, Deckert and Hejduk (2024) looked into whether spelling errors impact player satisfaction, *operationalised* with the use of the Game User Experience Satisfaction Scale (Keebler et al. 2020). They found that satisfaction – viewed as a composite construct – was lower in players who engaged with the version of the game that contained typos. Nonetheless, out of the nine factors that made up satisfaction as formulated in the experiment, an effect was found for just two: Usability/Playability and Personal Gratification.

As we construe VG access in line with the universalist view (Greco 2016), the scope is no longer limited to linguo-cultural backgrounds of users. When it comes to sensorial access provision that is linguistically mediated – if we take the criterion of language to operate as centripetal in the current volume – the prime solutions are subtitles for the deaf and the hard-of-hearing [SDH] and audio description [AD]. With respect to SDH, the research agenda that adopts a reception perspective largely remains to be set, with the aforementioned study by Mangiron (2016) being one study that sheds light on the matter with user data. By the same token, it is perhaps unexpected, especially given the amount of research that has been done into the reception of AD in the filmic context, that '[w]hile interest in game accessibility for the blind is gradually increasing from an engineering and game design perspective, until now research on the potential application of AD in video games has been almost non-existent' (Mangiron & Zhang 2016; Mangiron & Zhang 2022: 384). As Carme Mangiron and Xiaochun Zhang (2022: 384–385) go on to point out, one case that involves user-oriented work in game accessibility is the *Researching Audio Description* project conducted at Universitat Autònoma de Barcelona (cf. Larreina-Morales & Mangiron 2023). Another project investigating this topic is *AD4Games*: making VGs accessible for visually impaired players, based at the University of Bristol (Brigstow Institute 2021; cf. AD4Games 2021).

This overview indicates that while some valuable scholarly work has already been done that brings together VG translation and users, the research is still very limited and fragmented. The need for research is conspicuous if we juxtapose that research with what has been accomplished in reception studies that look into the experience of film viewers (cf. Di Giovanni & Gambier 2018). This area of AVT work used a wide range of methods, examining different translation modes, as well as different parameters of translation and the experiences of users (cf. e.g. Orrego-Carmona 2019; Di Giovanni 2020). Eyetracking applications alone date back to the 1980s (d'Ydewalle et al. 1985, 1987) and have been developing into a comprehensive body of work since (e.g. Perego 2012; see Kruger et al. 2015 for an overview). Evidently, the disproportion between film and game AVT reception cannot be accounted for by postulating that VGs are niche compared to films. Rather, it is more likely motivated by methodological considerations and very mundane limitations. Let us here refer to Mangiron's (2018a: 129; cf. Mangiron 2018b: 279) observation that:

> [...] despite the fact that one of the main tenets of game localisation – both from a theoretical and practical perspective – is that localised versions should provide players with a similar gameplay experience to those playing the original version, no studies have proven whether this is actually the case. Reception studies focusing on players' experience (PX) of both original and target players are few, due to the complexities associated with their design, obtaining subjects, and analysing data.

While a shift is both desired and beginning to emerge – as this volume intends to signal – the aforementioned observation appears to be especially pertinent to user-centred research in VGs translation modes other than subtitling. For instance, while dubbing in games has already received some research attention (Mejías-Climent 2022), no experimental study is known to the authors that probes the reception of dubbing in this context.

1.2 What Can Be Done – Researching AVT through UX

This Element tries to account for what can and needs to be done, mapping out – in a maximally comprehensive, although not necessarily exhaustive manner – the user-centred research into VG translation. As Ian Bogost writes in his book for media critics titled *How to Talk about Videogames* (2015: 3), the object of our study is 'operable' in that VGs 'do things, and the manner by which they do them matters. The result of their having been done matters. But the process and experience of that operation also matters'. He uses this as a demonstration that the medium must be 'more than just nondescript vessels that deliver [. . .] pleasure'. He reasons that the dimensions of VG experience must then extend beyond entertainment or distraction, like other media, since they too 'include characters and personas with whom we can identify and empathize', and show audiovisual forms of appeal that evoke 'feelings and emotions in us, just as art or music or fiction might do'. But VGs are also unique in having two sides (perhaps corresponding to a ludological and a narratological one): 'the functional, operative one [. . .] and the expressive formal one (the face that puts that operation in context)' (Bogost 2015: 4).

His observations are potent, because it is possible to subsume game localisation under what he abstractly calls 'the manner by which' VGs operate (Bogost 2015: 4). This marks one set of parameters or possible variables in game-localisation-user research, which we term the *facets of translated games*. Such facets function as decision-making points where more than one path can be followed – a canonical case being that of foreignisation and domestication (cf. Section 3), whereby elements like proper names can be rendered through translatorial choices on a spectrum from favouring to nullifying foreignness, as in the case of *Revelations: Persona*'s (Atlus 1996) character *Reiji* becoming *Chris* in the North American release.

Another set of *facets* is that of *user experience*. This set corresponds to the abstracted universals that Bogost (2015: 4) observed in what he called the experiential 'result' and the VG 'having been done'. This set of facets pertains to constructs representing the different dimensions of VG experience, as studied in reception research. In this sense, *facets of user experience* can be understood as measuring the effects that the VG has on its experiencers. An example would be designating an experimental variable measuring how immersed a user felt with the game world that had either been foreignised or domesticated,[1] as they interacted with it (cf. Section 2). Because the sets of facets discussed are interrelated, Bogost (2015: 4) seems to assert them as important for the analysis of the medium.

---

[1] The examples here purposefully allude to concepts that spark intrigue as long-lasting objects of media study but have been notoriously difficult to measure reliably (e.g. immersion, foreignness).

But as he also writes about 'the process and experience of that operation', we are reminded that the interpretative process is personal as it differs between the users – 'influenced by their sensory and cognitive abilities, as well as by their personality, experience and knowledge' (Bardini 2020: 259). Assuming that 'designing enjoyable and meaningful games requires [...] thinking about people's *experience* of games' (Ferrara 2012: 28), and considering the global and inclusive nature of contemporary gaming, we direct our attention to the *people* who experience the games, too. Thus, factors pertaining to users ought to be processed alongside their reception of VGs. Accepting this, we mark *facets of users* as our third and last set of variables relevant to the realistic study of VGs – for example how well a particular user of the game knows the source culture of that game (cf. Section 4) as they immerse themselves either in a foreignised or domesticated localisation. Viewing VG users as individuals, rather than a collective, facilitates more nuanced and methodical study of the contemporary (i.e. heavily heterogeneous) uses of VGs.

Such an orientation is consistent with the game-psychology determinants reported by Jari Takatalo, Jukka Häkkinen, Jyrki Kaistinen, and Göte Nyman (2010: 25–27). Among their compartments of users' internal psychology were 'cognition, emotion, motivation, perception, and attention' as well as more user-specific dimensions like 'past experiences (memories) and attitudes'. As these compartments become affected and shaped in the process of the users' contact with the game system (e.g. game-world setting, game-system interfaces), they can be used as 'lenses through which we observe the gamers' inner world', and even to 'reveal relevant determinants of the UX, such as its quality, intensity, meaning, value, and extensity'.

The three sets of *facets – user experience facets, translated game facets, and game users facets –* in our view represent dimensions of a realistic study of the characteristics of VG experiences in relation to the characteristics of VG localisation by monitoring how the profile of users (and perhaps even the researchers) can influence this relationship. It also clarifies the difference in perspective between looking at phenomena as a research *parameter*, a *variable*, and a *facet*. Our assumption is that all research has parameters that could be measured as variables (cf. *operationalisation*). But for the purpose of our blueprint (cf. Section 5) we grouped the parameters that pertain to game translation user research into three sets – turning each one of them into an individualised *facet* of game translation user research.

A related terminological–conceptual demarcation relevant for the research and industry fields this Element operates in (cf. Jiménez-Crespo 2018; Mangiron 2018: 124) is that of *localisation* vis a vis *translation*. One starting point for discussing this can be to realise that *localisation* is well established in the gaming industry as originating from internationalising software (O'Hagan 2005: 80). *Translation*, on the other hand, may appear as the primary term associated with academic Translation Studies – seemingly combining various operations performed by practitioners (e.g. *interpretation*). Thus, the question whether it is more appropriate to talk about *game localisation* (user research) or *game translation* (user research) has numerous relevant answers. As Mikołaj Deckert and Krzysztof W. Hejduk (2022a: 17) argued elsewhere:

> Solely focusing on the topic of VGs and software, the content-oriented distinctions between translation, screen translation, multimedial translation and transadaptation [...] can be contrasted with the more functional or macro-unit-oriented approaches of terms such as audiovisual translation and globalisation, or micro-unit-oriented terms like product localisation and culturalisation.

Since we generally adopt the vantage point of *audiovisual translation*, we feel compelled to choose *game translation user research* to refer to the general transfer of some qualities of multimodal texts from one setting onto another in accordance with their presumed functions. With this, *Game Translation User Research* becomes a possible name for an initiative related to (*Cognitive*) *Translation* (*and Interpretation*) *Studies* consistent with the paradigms detailed in *User-Centred Translation* (Suojanen et al. 2015). Still, to build a bridge between professional practice and scholarly research, hoping to find future synergies, we promote the inclusion of industry notions in the academic fields by utilising *(g)localisation* in this Element to mean a concrete product/ process: translation minding the presupposed needs of some target-customer market, within the frames of globalisation and internationalisation (like PR and marketing), the game publishing processes like *simultaneous shipment* (O'Hagan & Mangiron 2013: 112, 106, cf. O'Hagan & Mangiron 2004: 57), and standardised workflows (cf. Bernal-Merino 2015: 97; Bernal-Merino 2020: 298–300).

This Element aims to provide a cross-perspective overview of reception as a complex construct in research, from the point of view of possible conceptualisations of specific facets portraying various effects that the translated games can have on their users with the result of certain measurable experiences (possible dependent variables in translational research), alongside facets of the translated target texts (possible independent variables), and facets that characterise the VG recipients by minding the personal differences between them (possible independent, dependent, or moderating variables). Arguing that such research is severely underdeveloped and very much needed, we ultimately propose what could be called a blueprint, or a tentative map, in the sense that it outlines an emerging research area with examples of topics to be taken up. The proposal – as illustrated in Section 5 (Figure 16) not only draws on the three interrelated components: stimuli, receptors, and reaction, but also goes beyond this trichotomy. Notably, these notions are discussed in practical terms, with reference to instances of specific research questions based on the account in separate sections that follow, with the initiative to present actual practices, methods, and tools (Bernal-Merino 2016a) for capturing the relations between the three sets of *facets*. The studies reviewed in Section 2 go beyond VGs and into AVT and MA, discussing the reception of various modes and target texts. This is to appreciate the possibility of broadening the definition of audiovisual material to include gaming videos and interactive gameplay, nesting game localisation firmly in this domain. The three following sections will detail an account of *facets of user experience* (Section 2), *facets of the translated games* (Section 3), and *facets of game users* (Section 4).

2 Facets of User Experience

How can the reception of a localised VG be conceptualised? We can start by assuming that the *process* of play (experiencing a localised VG) mediates the emergence of some *product* in the form of reception (the effects of experiencing a localised VG). However, neither the process nor the product are unified phenomena that can be accessed or measured directly. We could, however, treat them as extensions or totalities of some measurable sub-phenomena. 'In psychometrics, measurement models include *latent variables* (i.e., those difficult to measure straightforwardly), which are measured with *observed variables* such as questionnaire items' (Takatalo et al. 2010: 33). This would allow us to glimpse into the process of experiencing a gameplay as a complex phenomenological structure consisting of several more discrete sub-experiences. The resulting reception can be thought of as a complex psychosocial *construct* made up of sub-constructs. The sub-constructs would reflect specific measurable effects that the localised VG has the potential to have on its experiencer. As a consequence, measuring constructs reflecting mental and behavioural phenomena can 'reveal determinants of the UX, such as its quality, intensity, meaning, value, and extensity' (Takatalo et al. 2010: 26).

To illustrate: play can induce states of 'tension or anxiety, and immersion within the game world' (Wiemeyer et al. 2016: 247). Naturally, just these three could never constitute a holistic picture of play experience, but they can represent some conceptual portion of it. These dimensions of reception can be measured in specific gameplay situations to be interpreted as results of localised gameplay and therefore *facets of user experience*. As Wiemeyer et al. (2016: 247) put it, 'the effects of any one system element on the entire player experience is composed of an intricate collection of relationships between the factors defining [player experience]'. This points to another thing to remember while researching psychosocial-constructs conglomerates: their constituents might be interrelated with one another. For instance, certain experiential concepts can overlap in their characteristics (e.g. immersion, flow, engagement). Moreover, VG reception effects are subjective in the sense that, depending on the *facets of game user*, VG receptors respond differently or more intensely to different kinds of experiences. While some would be especially thrilled by reading character dialogues, others would rather explore the game-world environment. For this reason, monitoring respondent-specific variables (e.g. their motivation and their language proficiency) can expose more intricate connections between phenomena during analysis (cf. Section 4 on *facets of game users*).

Depending on the framing of reception, researchers could undertake the study of dimensions that go beyond the scope of this Element, but nonetheless inevitably point to the role and potential of translation in medium-user interactions for a global medium like VGs. For instance, by defining reception in terms of sales, researchers of VGs in international and translational contexts ought to consider how well a given product performs on the (local) market and how that may relate to other degrees of reception and *facets of user experience* – for example asking questions like *how well does it fulfil users' needs for its price? how much are users willing to pay?* etc. From a more practical perspective, another line of work could look into all kinds of lasting effects that VGs have on users, asking questions like *what therapeutic or educational or activistic values can it hold for users?* etc. Taken together, these avenues might however turn into critical discourse – aiming to heighten customers' demands or expectations. As we acknowledge that reception is a very broad concept, the following sub-sections cannot aim for an exhaustive account, but we wish to provide an illustration of research tendencies comprehensive enough to become useful for future discussions of user-centred localisation research.

2.1 Designing Game Translation User Research

Games Research and User Experience [GRUX] is a group affiliated with IGDA,[2] facilitating the flow of information between companies creating VGs,

---

[2] IGDA (International Game Developers Association 2020), formerly Computer Game Developers Association, is a 'global network of collaborative communities and individuals from all fields of

their consultants, and UX researchers. The group 'focuses on players' psychology and their behaviour' by utilising rigorous methodologies that include but go beyond playtesting, in order to 'help provide players with the best gaming experience possible' (IGDA Games Research and User Experience SIG 2023). They set out to improve VG experiences by facilitating Game User Research (GUR; Drachen et al. 2018: 3) and Player Experience [PX] work, which is why the group consists of developers, specialists, and researchers in VG-adjacent fields. One of the resources endorsed by them (IGDA Games Research and User Experience SIG 2023) is a website dedicated to publicising 'methods used to evaluate the playability and usability of games', maintained by the GUII [Game User Interaction and Intelligence] research lab at the University of California, Santa Cruz. At the time of writing, the website dedicates entries overviewing the think-aloud protocol, retrospective testing, heuristic evaluation, game analytics, playtesting and physiology-based playtesting, as well as ethnography, day reconstruction method, and three variants of ecological momentary assessment (experience sampling, refined experience sampling, event-contingent experience sampling). They also recommend tools for physiological measurements and multimethodological platforms featuring eyetracking, biometric signals (e.g. galvanic skin response, cardiography, encephalography), surveys, facial expression recognition, and other sensors. Above all, however, they provide instructions on the analysis and reporting of GUR, both in terms of analysis of qualitative and quantitative data.

Research design maps phenomena using variables. Variables can hold descriptive or numerical data values, corresponding to the responses users may give to, respectively, more open-ended or more close-ended questions. Both types of insight into reception are useful, and they can be paired (cf. Babbie 2021: 24–26). If users are given room to express themselves, their answers can provide researchers with valuable data that might not adhere to what the researchers had anticipated to elicit, allowing for more accurate or realistic findings. Nonetheless, collecting data from large samples of respondents may necessitate a more rigid structure of the reception probing methodology. The researchers could for example ask users to rate their subjective game experiences on a scale from one to seven (*Likert-type scales*) – each extreme representing polar-opposite responses, for example 'very much' or 'not at all' (*response anchors*). This and certain other types of data can be aggregated and submitted to *statistical hypothesis testing* – a standard procedure in psychometrics.

---

game development' tied to the origins of GDC [Game Developers Conference]. Other IGDA groups besides GRUX include Anti-Censorship/Social Issues, Quality Assurance, Localisation (LocSIG), and Accessibility (GA-SIG).

For analysing quantitative data, Game User Interaction and Intelligence Lab (2022) guidelines involve processes like identifying data types, performing descriptive statistics, and then testing hypotheses using statistical calculations. Data types can be identified according to this list:

- Nominal data – for example users' genders, VGs' genres (only mode is calculable),
- Ordinal data – for example VG's degree of domestication (most common descriptive statistics are calculable for these data sets, except for example standard deviation),
- Interval data – for example narrative-comprehension test scores,
- Ratio data – for example users' age values.

Identification of data types is crucial for choosing the right type of parametric statistical test. The GUII lab guidelines survey some of them, like the within-subjects and between-subjects t-tests (they compare two samples of non-nominal data), ANOVA (compares more than two samples of non-nominal data), and chi-squared (compares more than one samples of nominal data). Some non-parametric equivalents are also surveyed, like the Mann–Whitney–Wilcoxon's test (compares two samples of between-subjects non-nominal data) or Kruskal–Wallis' one-way ANOVA on ranks (compares more than two samples of non-nominal data).

For qualitative content, Game User Interaction and Intelligence Lab (2022), based on Hsieh and Shannon's paper (2005), recommends three approaches to interviewing: conventional, directed, or summative. The conventional approach is described as suitable for developing new theories, much like Grounded Theory (cf. Brown & Cairns 2004). The directed approach, contrarily, is advised for conceptually extending existing theoretical frameworks. In both approaches, the procedure starts with repeatedly studying the interviews conducted – with open-ended questions and upon informed consent – while taking notes and identifying themes and keywords, *coding* them. Coding is a process of systematic pattern-finding in a set of typically transcribed interviews, although some notable risks associated with it include decontextualising and overinterpreting data (St. Pierre & Jackson 2014: 716). Whence, setting an adequate degree of *dependability* (cf. Phakiti 2015: 31) is necessary for developing findings that accurately represent data, which 'can be established through […] debriefing, prolonged engagement, persistent observation, triangulation, negative case analysis, referential adequacy, and member checks' as well as showing that 'textual evidence is consistent with the interpretation' (Hsieh & Shannon 2005: 1280, 1285). In the conventional approach, the codes are subsequently categorised and organised into clusters with definitions. In the direct approach, the coding scheme is different, since both the variables and their operational definitions originate from existing theories, not the data (Hsieh & Shannon 2005: 1281). The summative approach investigates usage based on samples of communication events (Hsieh & Shannon 2005: 1283–1284), for example by quantifying the frequencies of key phrases that occur in the data set (including any identified semantic equivalents, like euphemisms).

To ensure research validity and actionable operability, but also to spare researchers the work of generating survey questions themselves, a selection of reliable, psychometrically validated questionnaires with ready-made items is also provided by the guidelines (Game User Interaction and Intelligence Lab 2022) to be utilised in UX self-report gathering. Importantly, each recommended instrument corresponds with certain (sets of) phenomena related to play reception, for example intrinsic motivation to consume VGs, feelings and affects, absorption in the game world, social interaction. One specialised instrument is even dedicated to studying non-player users: a five-construct scale named *Measuring Audience Experience* including the dimensions of enjoyment, mood, game engagement, social engagement, and perceived participation (Downs et al. 2013). Some instruments seem to even be designed as multifunctional, with some cross-construct triangulation in mind, like the *Presence Questionnaire*'s (Witmer & Singer 1998) measuring the reception of control and responsiveness of a game, its communication modalities, play meaningfulness, and attention distribution; or the *Player Experience Inventory* that measures PX at 'both the level of Functional[3] and Psychosocial consequences' (Abeele et al. 2020: 11, 9). The breadth of specialised instruments implies that researchers need to define (Babbie 2021: 43–44) which aspects of experience they can investigate, minding the possibility of *respondent fatigue*. In other words, a study needs to firstly concretise what constitutes whatever is being investigated (*conceptualisation*) and how it will be measured (*operationalisation*). The measurement can be undertaken with the aforementioned psychometric scales and instruments, as per GRUX recommendations (Game User Interaction and Intelligence Lab 2022).

The following subsections overview a selection of ways in which scholars conceptualise and operationalise what we call *facets of user experience* as they are related to the reception of audiovisual target texts, including VGs. For ease of exposition, these receptive facets as presented in the subsections below are semi-arbitrarily grouped by us into related categories. Studies into AVT and MA have been using designs that inspect experiential dimensions across the groups that we propose here – for example questionnaire studies cuing participants with

---

[3] 'the immediate, direct experience of game mechanics' (Haider et al. 2022: 18).

AVT material and asking them to self-report on emotional response, comprehension, satisfaction, and the evaluation of the translation format (e.g. Bardini 2020: 265). While this approximation serves to make the constructs less abstract, we must explicitly acknowledge that we are not suggesting that the clusters be studied as joint constructs, or investigated one in substitution of another. This is also why the level of detail in the descriptions of studies in the subsections that follow is at the Element's highest, as it serves the purpose of exemplifying specific procedures undertaken by a non-exhaustive choice of model scholars in the relevant domains of studies.

2.2 Immersion, Absorption, Presence, Transportation, Flow

One of the first lines of work trying to investigate the fundamental constructs of VG experience was *immersion*. Its name is a metaphor of the instinctual feeling of absorption and being intensely submerged in the development of the virtual events of the VGs, much like its counter-construct *emersion* (Kubiński 2014). Despite the terms' popularity, both inside and outside of VG discourse, it remains vague and mostly rooted either in intuitive receptive feelings or prejudices about the kinds of effects that the medium is known to have on its users. In other words, it is unclear 'what exactly is meant by immersion and indeed even whether the different research on immersion is talking about the same concept' (Brown & Cairns 2004: 1297). Elisa Perego, Fabio Del Missier, and Sara Bottiroli (2015: 16–17) conceptualised psychological immersion as an experience different from presence (feeling present in the film's diegesis; 'being spatially located in the mediated environment'), transportation (narrative engagement; 'being mentally drawn away from the actual physical environment into the world of narrative'), and flow ('being intensely involved in and focused on a given activity to the extent of losing self-consciousness') as well as enjoyment ('appreciation, attraction, preference'). Nurit Tal-Or and Jonathan Cohen (2010: 403–404) moreover particularise concepts like identification (empathetic affinity with story characters), for which they found evidence that it might be different from transportation, although similar in involving a degree of presence: 'a loss of awareness of the viewing situation and a shift in identity'. An example they gave is the portrayal of 'negative heroes' in media, whose reception might resist identification, but elicit *suspense* and *transportation*. They moreover differentiate those mental states from the state of *flow* (Csikszentmihalyi 1990), which denotes a kind of deep focus on the 'immediate reality' rather than 'alternative reality' (Tal-Or & Cohen 2010: 405).

Furthermore, the researchers ascribe to the experiencers exposed to states of heightened involvement the capacity to react as observers, participants, or both – and not necessarily involving a positive response. This last observation is fascinating for the possibility of investigating similar concepts in the (localisations of) the interactive medium, which allows players to participate in the stories and the development of characters. It points to the potential of studying how stable, across language versions, the character integrity is when relayed in localisation, considering the artistic and persuasive qualities of *procedural-rhetoric* mechanisms (Bogost 2011: 11–14; Sterczewski 2012). An immediately relevant example would be for example putting the player in the (intentionally uncomfortable) role of a villain character or an anti-hero (cf. e.g. series like *Grand Theft Auto*; *The Last of Us*), or enabling the player to determine their avatar's/the protagonist's morality (cf. *alignment* in RPGs). For comparison, Hugh W. Nettelbeck (2020: 66) detected asymmetrical perceptions of a film character's personality suggesting that reliance on interlingual-translation subtitling could, to a degree, functionally reshape how users view characters based on locale. This creates opportunities for VG-user reception research in terms of *facets of translated games* and how equivalent the portrayal of characters is between source and targets – transferring of characterisation, idiolects, and the programming of player avatars as originally intended by the developers.

2.2.1 Dissecting An Example: Game-World Engagement Research

For the purposes of dissecting an example of VG user-oriented research into player-involvement constructs, let us consider one that constitutes the forerunning of empirical VG-reception works. Emily Brown and Paul Cairns (2004) set out to illuminate some unanswered questions regarding the evanescent idea of VG immersion and its related (sub)constructs. They conducted semi-structured interviews with VG players about this experiential dimension, then analysed the data with the Grounded Theory method. Their recognition of the values of user-centred research was fruitful, giving them insight into immersion as a phenomenon possibly encompassing sub-experiences, or 'different levels of engagement with a game' (Brown & Cairns 2004: 1297). The sample of participants involved seven regular gameplayers (four men, three women) above the age of 18, all 'English speakers' – presumably native, although this is left unstated (Brown & Cairns 2004: 1298). The study first stimulated/primed participants with a 30-minutes play of 'their favourite game[s]'. This was to elicit participants' own, custom experiences of immersion, but also to spur them to introspect, contemplating 'what it is that they enjoy about gaming' on a potent example of the VGs that they most prefer. Following this pre-task, participants were asked about certain qualities of immersion (sense of *presence*, awareness of time). The researchers also specifically mention taking due care to avoid *response bias* – putting 'words into the interviewees' mouths' (cues that could influence their participants' responses). They also comment that participants were initially videoed while they played the VGs to isolate any behavioural patterns associated with immersion, but this multi-method was discontinued once the researchers observed 'little physical action of any sort' from the respondents.

Overall, the study revealed some intricate dynamics between immersive states and other aspects of gameplay (Brown & Cairns 2004: 1298–1299). For one, they characterised immersion as a charged phenomenon, possibly conditioned by elements like game aesthetics, fair balance between challenges and payoffs, and even interesting narrations. Secondly, they also defined some barriers to immersive experiences (Brown & Cairns 2004: 1298–1299). The representation of users' control over the VG, their willingness to invest time, and their ability to concentrate were also described as potentially being at play for feeling immersed. Emotional investment, escapism, suspension of disbelief, and empathy were also suggested for further studies on feelings of absorption by the game and presence in the game world. The study (Brown & Cairns 2004: 1300) even details some parallels as well as differences between immersion and the psychological construct of flow (Csikszentmihalyi 1990). All this cemented the idea that immersion is both a 'shared concept' and 'not a static experience', opening new avenues for decades of future research. Indeed, Wiemeyer, Nacke, Moster, and Mueller (2016: 250–251) years later presented immersion as a phenomenon possibly incorporating flow and presence, constructs that themselves would consist of sub-factors: spatial/physical presence as they report would be conditioned by 'involvement and suspension of disbelief', but first by attentional processes, both user- and media-dependent.

2.3 Attention, Cognitive Load, Comprehension, Memory

Among other reasons, a target version of a VG could be labelled as inadequate if it happens to result in negative experiences that are asymmetrical compared to the source version. One example would involve exposing the VG user to unnecessary effort as a result of translational choices. In the context of processing audiovisual information in order to learn and adapt, not too dissimilar to that of gaming, cognitive overloads can lead to unintended negative emotional states, like frustration and/or dissatisfaction (Kruger et al. 2013: 62). To substantiate this, let us consider an example of user interface elements designed to be intuitive for users, yet which fail to be so in the target-language version of the software – straining users to comprehend what was supposed to be easy for them. As a result, investigating how effortful or processing-intensive certain *facets of translated games* are appears to be one of the most natural opportunities for research, because often it can be thought of as nearly directly demonstrating the quality of a given language version.

One way to measure this is through eyetracking (cf. Kruger 2019). In the domain of VG studies, Samuel Almeida, Ana Veloso, Licinio Roque, and Oscar Mealha (2011) prepared a review of how eye-gaze tracking is used as an instrument in VG analysis and evaluation. Depending on game-specific facets like the genre of the game (cf. Section 3 on *facets of translated games*) and characteristics of player motivations (cf. Section 4 *on facets of game users*), players would be variously interested in the kinds of information offered by the multimodal material. Each stimulus, including the kinds of visual prompts available in the channels perceived by the eyes (cf. e.g. Zabalbeascoa 2008), competes for the users' attention. The way eyetracking provides researchers with insight into the subjects' attentional processes, i.a. of VG users (cf. Kudła 2020), is predicated on 'human's capacity to process' sensory information (including visual), which is limited in the context of large amounts of stimuli available for access. This results in *selective attention* – a typically involuntary filtering process, to the point of sometimes being incidental, but nonetheless generally assumed to be a reflexive sign of attentional processes (Almeida et al. 2011: 2). For instance, if a user's gaze – as captured by the eyetracking system – explores a visual environment and then *fixates* on a particular element for a calculable amount of time, this is interpreted as an indication of the user focusing their attention to process whatever they chose to see. In the context of subtitle length in translated audiovisual material, a more potent example – and one that is easily translatable into for example game-cinematics localisation – is the eye-gaze measurement of cognitive load as exhibited by longer fixation durations and reading times, as well as greater counts of revisits and fixations (Szarkowska & Gerber-Morón 2018: 12–13).

2.3.1 Dissecting An Example: Cognitive Processing Research

A study by Jan-Louis Kruger, Esté Hefer, and Gordon Matthew (2014) shows another example of how to tap into such latent mental responses in the context of AVT. It should be noted that the study focuses not on interactive VGs, but on studying educational video materials. Nevertheless, the experimental setup of their study is referenced here because of how it can be adapted to suit translated-games users studies. Their design mixes subjective and objective measures, utilising three methods: eyetracking (presumably combined with screen-recording and key-logging), electro-encephalography, and a structured meta-cognitive questionnaire. Their participants were stimulated with a recording of an academic lecture, with the aim 'to determine the impact of attention distribution and subtitle language on comprehension in an academic context, and to determine the impact of subtitles on cognitive load' (Kruger et al. 2014: 1). As aforementioned, the possibility of mental constructs working in related fashion cannot be ruled out, so the scholars probed both cognitive capacities and memory resources of their 72 respondents. Equally, measures of *user facets* were collected to 'control for confounding variables such as age, field of study, and existing knowledge' (Kruger et al. 2014: 4, cf. Section 4).

Participants of the study were randomly assigned to three groups. Depending on the group, under eyetracking with EEG indexing, they watched one of three versions of audiovisual material with different properties of the subtitles. More precisely, the manipulated independent variable was the mode of AVT (cf. Section 3 on *facets of translated games*): group A watched a video without subtitles, group B watched the same video with source-language subtitles, and group C watched it with target-language subtitles. Other parameters of the audiovisual material were not variable between groups: dubbing was audible in the source-language, all subtitles used a maximum of two lines, up to 37 characters each, at a reading speed (*presentation rate*) of 120 word per minute, with non-dialogue *on-screen language* left untranslated (Kruger et al. 2014: 4). The eyetracking measurements as utilised by the scholars included calculations of the percentage of 'time spent looking at and processing' (*dwell time*) the subtitles (*areas of interest*) compared to gazing upon any other parts of the screen (Kruger et al. 2014: 5–6). Measures like 'mean fixation duration and fixation count are less useful in the context of [...] reading', since it elicits numerous short fixations due to the process of reading itself, compared to for example picture-gazing (Kruger et al. 2013: 63). On another practical note, the researchers had conducted filtration of invalid data and found four sets to be disqualifiable as they did not meet the required eyetracking cut-off point of 80 per cent ratio of eye movement being tracked (Kruger et al. 2014: 4).

Their other measurements, as equally available for VG studies, included self-reports, test scoring, and electroencephalography. The scalp-electrodes EEG measured the emitted brain-wave activity patterns, of which Alpha and Theta wave-rhythms were interpreted in terms of five attentional categories: excitement (short-term, long-term), frustration, engagement, and meditation (Kruger et al. 2014: 6, 7). All groups also self-reported, through a questionnaire, some measures of cognitive effort: how mentally demanding, temporally rushed, frustrating, difficult to understand, and concentration-intensive the task had seemed for them (Kruger et al. 2014: 5). The operational definition of comprehension performance as used by Kruger et al. (2014: 9) was the success-rates on a comprehension exam, asking questions about the content and form of the presented audiovisual material. To be more precise, it was the ratio of correct to incorrect answers each group scored.

The comprehension test as used by Kruger et al. (2014: 9) was issued directly post-task (short-term memory) and two weeks later (long-term memory) to examine how well the participants understood the audiovisual material. The test consisted of multiple choice questions, suggesting that *recall* was not tested. A different battery of memory-performance metrics was utilised by Elisa Perego, Fabio Del Missier, and Sara Bottiroli (2015: 5–6) to encompass 'both visual and verbal aspects of performance' (cf. Szarkowska & Gerber-Morón 2018: 11, 19):

- dialogue recognition (possible question: *has this phrase been uttered in the video?*),
- visual scene recognition (ditto: *has this freeze-frame been a part of the video?*),
- name-face association (ditto: *what was the name of this character?*).

They moreover investigated how cognitively taxing the processing of target texts might be from the perspective of users' age. To control for the individual differences between the participants studied (cf. Section 4 on *facets of game users*) they used indicators of respondents' fluid intelligence, processing speed, episodic memory, and sensory decline, using specialised cognitive tests, tasks, and puzzles (Perego et al. 2015: 3, 10).

Similar design setups to that of Kruger et al. (2014) and Perego et al. (2015) can be undertaken for example to gain insight into the effects of different modes of VG translation, like subtitles whose speed is controlled by the player. Eyetracking can also be used to identify cognitive load levels more directly, by comparing the blinking rates per minute in game users when they interact with different difficulty-levels in a VG, as evidenced by Lagunes-Ramirez, González-Serna, Lopez-Sánchez, Fragoso-Díaz, Castro-Sánchez, and Olivares-Rojas (2020). Kruger et al. (2013: 62–63) moreover showed that high cognitive effort could be operationalised via eyetracking through the indexing of pupil dilation increases, although they do note that the 'numerous external factors' (*confounding variables*) that have the potential to influence pupillometry limit its effectiveness.

All of the aforementioned techniques are viable options for game localisation reception studies. To exemplify, existing studies incorporating eyetracking in particular in the context of game localisation reception already includes papers by Mangiron (2016) and Kudła (2020). Future researchers can apply methods like comprehension tests, monitoring of player gaze, and self-reports to investigate aspects of play on a global scale such as *diegetic on-screen language* texture localisation (cf. Deckert & Hejduk 2022a; Hejduk 2022), UI texts placement and text overflow, dubbing/subtitle properties (speed, length, number of lines . . .) and especially game accessibility, including the growing potential of audio-description application in VGs (Mangiron & Zhang 2022: 384; Larreina-Morales & Mangiron 2023) – in and out of cinematics (AD4Games 2021) – and how target versions could be improved in each of these terms.

2.4 Affective Response, Feelings, Perceived Funniness

Despite its importance – i.a. for reception studies – the term *emotion* has been notoriously difficult to define as a unified phenomenon (cf. Frijda 2007a) and for long had even been considered as impossible to measure reliably (Ramos 2015: 71). Nevertheless, finding definitions that are 'flexible' and 'capable of development' – 'pragmatic tools in the search for intensions' – can help establish common grounds for 'communication among researchers' and allow room for discussions (Frijda 2007b: 434). While scholars generally agree that emotions 'have an infrastructure that includes neural systems' (Izard 2009: 6) or that emotions interact with cognition (Izard 2009: 20), emotions 'defied definition' mainly because of their nature as non-unitary qualia (Izard 2009: 3–4). Moreover, some of the more complex emotional states can even be conditioned by 'the knowledge of cultural rules and appropriate behaviour' (Matamala et al. 2020: 132). This appears heavily related to what can be termed emotive *schemas*, which for similar reasons tend to 'differ across individuals and cultures' (Izard 2009: 6).

There are two major ways to classify emotions (Matamala et al. 2020: 132). 'Most emotion theories distinguish between two basic concepts: discrete states of emotion (often referred to as basic emotions [. . .]) or biphasic emotional dimensions' (Wiemeyer et al. 2016: 259). Examples of basic emotions would include happiness, surprise, anger, '[y]et, the identification of these basic emotions has been proved rather controversial' (Matamala et al. 2020: 132). Biphasic emotional dimensions, on the other hand, 'often differentiate between positive and negative, appetitive and aversive' (Wiemeyer et al. 2016: 259), or '[p]hysical activation or arousal', which can be high or low (Matamala et al. 2020: 132). In this way, a related psychological construct is that of *affective valence*. Notably, if emotions are central to the experience of films (cf. Ramos 2016: 607) and drive people toward audiovisual experiences, for example by mediating the exposure users have to the game-machine, then felt emotions must constitute a variable in comprehensive game reception research. Thus, emotions are compound phenomena that are difficult to conceptualise as a unit to be studied.

In order to be able to measure emotions through bodily signs, a researcher needs to assume that affective processes are connected with physiological processes. In other words, an assumption is made that emotions can manifest psycho-physiologically as a result of using VGs (Wiemeyer et al. 2016: 260), for example in blood pressure and heart rate (cf. Rojo et al. 2014). Wiemeyer et al. (2016: 260) remark that measuring this kind of data (e.g. through ECG wearables like wristbands) is seen as very objective, because it is generated by participants, in a sense, involuntarily. However, for the same reason, it can also be difficult to interpret correctly. There is a risk of confounding variables influencing the data. An example given by Wiemeyer et al. (2016: 260) is participants talking during the study, which might result in the quickening of their pulses. This also suggests that a physiological response, reliable as it might be, could mean different things: mental processes are 'not always in a direct relationship to the underlying brain response'; 'we cannot map physiological responses directly to a discrete emotional state' (Wiemeyer et al. 2016: 260). Since physiological signals can potentially arise from variables other than the ones defined by the study, experimenters investigating emotions are advised to conduct studies in a 'controlled experimental environment'.

2.4.1 Dissecting an Example: Emotional States Research

In the realm of media accessibility, Marina Ramos (2015: 73) reported a reception study testing the emotional experience of disgust, fear, sadness (chosen as easiest to induce in a laboratory setting through validated filmic scenes) in sighted audiences versus those with visual impairments. 'All blind participants were completely blind: some were congenitally blind and the rest acquired blindness' (Ramos 2015: 72). Other parameters of the subjects as controlled for by the study (cf. Section 4 on *facets of game users*) included socio-economic background, education, preferences, women's menstrual cycle day, and even smoking habits since those could influence the results of the study (Ramos 2015: 73). Participants can also be given control over the sound volume of the test stimuli (Ramos 2015: 72) to control for differences in their hearing capacity and make the experience more natural for them.

The study's methodology utilised both a more subjective and a more objective measurement of emotional response: an introspective Likert-questionnaire instrument combined with heart activity monitoring. Similar types of designs operating with apparatuses measuring physiological and biochemical signals can be utilised in studies of VG dubbing and accessibility features designed to provide access to VGs or eliminate sensory and cognitive barriers to them. For one, '[h]eart rate is an indicator of emotions that is relatively inexpensive and easy to measure, while providing information that can be related to differences in the intensity' of feelings (Ramos 2015: 72). On a practical note, the participants of such tests should be asked to relax before the task. Similarly, between presenting participants with the stimuli, a recovery period of a few minutes for relaxation, performing a side-task, or a *catch trial* can be planned to 'extinguish the emotional response produced by the previous stimulus, before the presentation of a new one' (Matamala et al. 2020: 135).

When it comes to the questionnaire method, Ramos' study (2015: 75) simply asked participants to evaluate on a scale, pre-task and post-task, the extent to which they felt certain emotions and response states (alertness, agitation, anxiety). A similar approach was taken by Bardini (2020: 270), comparing different formats in terms of effects on joy, attraction, interest, as well as more meta-cognitive dimensions like the enjoyment of access to an enjoyable experience and a film's aesthetics. The participants evaluated the intensity of the corresponding *facets of user experience* on summative Likert scales (1–6 without a neutral option) at a selection of key moments of their viewing of the stimulus material (Bardini 2020: 270–272). This method can prove useful in reception studies investigating all kinds of *translational facets* of VGs – from participants self-reporting how emotional (if reliably operationsalised) they felt upon reading translated poetry, or upon hearing localised dubbing of VGs, to how funny they found the game characters, events, jokes, or the plot in the localised version.

Indeed, another relevant dimension of this subset of user experience facets, useful for between-title and between-user comparisons, is trying to grasp how a translated game manages to be funny (Mangiron 2010; O'Hagan & Flanagan 2018) – to what extent users believe the localisation fulfils the perlocutionary humorous functions of the game (cf. *skopos*). As Mangiron (2010: 91–92) observes, humour has been recognised as performing meaningful roles in VGs, potentially facilitating enjoyment (element of surprise), relief of tension (cf. *cognitive load*), sense of belonging, engagement or involvement, narratives (characterisation, interactions between characters), relating to characters, and that it generally supports gameplay. Thus, it should not be overlooked as an aspect of the ludic experience of VGs. Observation of participants, noting their bursts of laughter, or facial expressions, as well as interviewing them, or surveying with Likert-type scales can all be exercised in the investigation of affect-oriented subsets of *facets*.

It should also be mentioned that AVT and MA research into affective reactions has been utilising other physiological measurements (Ramos 2015: 72) like electro-dermal activity (cf. Matamala et al. 2020 for an overview) and hormonal secretions (e.g. cortisol levels). Moreover, employing a case-study-like analysis of the texts (e.g. through multimodal analysis tools) alongside the presentation of reception results can allow researchers to deconstruct the mechanisms employed by film/game makers to trigger emotional or immersive effects in audiences – cues like salience, setting, *mise-en-scene*, lighting (Ramos 2015: 88, 70). A relevant mechanism here is that of *emotional contagion*, whereby media recipients empathise with a character they witness in an automatic way, 'i.e. without cognitive mediation' (Ramos 2015: 71). Naturally, these also apply to VG *cutscenes* or more cinematic, linear gameplay segments, but a similar phenomenon to be further studied in more canonical gameplaying would be that of players narratively embodying their in-game avatars, co-creating their own unique storylines in their heads, with affective states being induced by the game world (Patridge 2017).

2.5 Satisfaction, Enjoyment, Fun

Satisfaction can be conceptualised as a 'multidimensional construct that involves different dimensions', although the exact number and qualities of these dimensions are somewhat fuzzy and controversial among VG scholars, users, and even creators (Phan et al. 2016: 1218). Components of VG satisfaction can encompass fun, aesthetics, choice, freedom, usability, motivation, engagement, presence, and other aspects relying on the individuals' interests or the particular idea behind the given creation. Indeed, Tal-Or and Cohen (2010: 414) found that enjoyment was predicated on transportation (although they admit these findings may not be generalisable across all text types), employing the operationalisation of enjoyment in three questions: if participants enjoyed their experience, if they would be likely to participate in it if given the chance, and if they thought that the creation could be enjoyable to them (Tal-Or & Cohen 2010: 410). For VGs, the relations between enjoyment and involvement-related constructs might be even more exacerbated due to their participation-oriented nature.

In any case, the enjoyment or satisfaction that users have with audiovisual creations is a crucial statistic for the consumers, reviewers, and distribution platforms. Just to illustrate, both Steam and Epic Games platforms employ player-data to make potential customers aware of the value that other clients placed on their experiences with a given VG title. At the same time, entire websites are dedicated to quantifying input from users or experts, then standardising and comparing how well similar or different VG titles performed in terms of the price to quality ratio. One constant, however, is that the positive evaluation of VGs hinges on high-quality translations so that the VG is sold internationally and experienced adequately regardless of language barriers. Yet, and perhaps because of the highly globalised state of gaming, these industry metrics hardly seem to account for the fact that the opinions they collect originate from different language versions. Instead, they treat them homogenously. An optimistic interpretation of this would likely be that this might be an indication of general appreciation and a global recognition of the work that localisers undertake to provide each and all users with quality VGs offering experiences that are as symmetrical between locales as possible (Bernal-Merino 2016b), regardless of language and accessibility issues.

Thus, it is no wonder that translation and localisation experts try to investigate the enjoyment of media as yet another *facet of user experience*. Agnieszka Szarkowska and Olivia Gerber-Morón (2018: 5), for the purposes of their film-translation reception study, conceptualised enjoyment as a construct encompassing both hedonic needs (states of pleasure) as well as non-hedonic needs (satisfactory translational parameters), assuming that the sense of enjoyment is predicated on some level of UX quality, like manageable presentation rate of subtitles. In comparison, regarding a non-translation VG study, Harteveld et al. (2020: 4) saw satisfaction as 'more than enjoyment', as it can encompass the value that users see in playing a VG and i.a. learning something through that.

This interestingly corresponds with the literature review conducted by Elisa Perego, Fabio Del Missier, and Sara Bottiroli (2015: 2–3), which presented two positions, either relating the users' appreciation of translational modes to them experiencing immersion (posing that certain modes might support the authentic atmosphere or ambient mood of the audiovisual material better) or not experiencing cognitive overload (posing that certain modes of translation might disrupt the intended composition of the audiovisual material). Their findings ultimately undermined the latter position (Perego et al. 2015: 15), but found some limited confirmatory evidence for the former. In their study, participants were first randomly assigned to two experimental conditions. In this study, both groups viewed the same film, but the experimental manipulation was the translation mode: either dubbing or subtitles, professionally applied to a commercial-film release (Perego et al. 2015: 5). Such a setup ensured high construct validity for a prototypical audiovisual target text excerpt, though it also points to the possibility in localised-game user research to investigate other, perhaps less prototypical, parameters of dubbing/voice-over and subtitling (e.g. position, colour, background). Moreover, while participants exhibited similar appreciation of the film regardless of the AVT mode in their study, Perego et al. (2015: 14) found that the subtitled version of the film tended to be preferred more by older adults. With that, new horizons are opened for dedicated research into the qualities of different modes of game translation, especially for senior VG players/viewers.

2.5.1 Dissecting an Example: Play Quality Research

One increasingly viable way of measuring how satisfying a VG (localisation) is for its users would be employing psychometrically validated scales. The concept of *playtesting* usually consists of administering questionnaires to testers after their gameplay to estimate the expectations of the target population and whether or not the intentions behind the VG were realised in practice. This time-constrained environment necessitates the preference for effective instruments which balance brevity with a multifaceted measurement of satisfaction. A good example would be Vero Vanden Abeele, Katta Spiel, Lennart Nacke, Daniel Johnson, and Kathrin Gerling's (2020) Player Experience Inventory (PXI). It is a reliable tool for measuring the users' own evaluation of *facets of user experience* like a game's meaningfulness, feedback, immersion, freedom, curiosity, mastery, challenge, audiovisual appeal, ease of control, and clarity of rules. Scholars have already preliminarily attempted to shorten this robust scale to just a dozen items, while simultaneously extending it to include the umbrella *facet* of enjoyment. The truncated scale under the name Mini Player Experience Inventory (mPXI, later miniPXI) however remains to be adjusted so as not to offer significantly compromised effectiveness due to the reduced number of items (Harteveld 2020; Haider et al. 2022).

Another psychometric instrument, the Game User Experience Satisfaction Scale (GUESS) is reported in a paper by Mikki Phan, Joseph Keebler, and Barbara Chaparro (2016: 1217–1218), which explains that the scale was developed and validated in the context of ameliorating the lack of consensus about what constitutes the 'crucial building blocks of highly satisfying game[s]'. Noticing the need for comprehensive psychometric tools for assessing the overall satisfaction in different dimensions of user experience across VGs, the authors (Phan et al. 2016: 1220) first determine those dimensions, then combine them into one reliable instrument. Their definition of VG satisfaction is how much the user feels gratified with the experience. The final set of items reflected the compound factors of (Phan et al. 2016: 1238):

- playability (intuitive play, clarity of goals, fluent use of interface and controls),
- narratives (interesting and emotion-shaping story and characters),
- engrossment (play that captures and holds the attention),
- enjoyment (pleasure and delight as a perceived result of play),
- creative freedom (fostering of curiosity, freedom to express oneself),
- audio aesthetics (how much auditory aspects enriched the experience),
- video aesthetics (how attractive the graphics were in the respondents' opinion),
- personal gratification (sense of accomplishment, motivation to continue),
- and social connectivity (features that facilitate social connection).

The scale can be used to assess overall satisfaction in a variety of game genres, as well as to gain 'insight as to what factors contribute' the most (Phan et al. 2016: 1243). The original large pool of items was truncated in a later study by Joseph Keebler, William Shelstad, Dustin Smith, Barbara Chaparro, and Mikki Phan (2020: 53, 62) to a model consisting of just 18 Likert items (known as GUESS-18), which 'can be completed in as little as a few minutes and can be used to assess game perceptions over time or for cross-game comparisons' (Keebler et al. 2020: 58). The GUESS and GUESS-18 can thus be used to contrast the psychometric sub-constructs of satisfaction (as aggregable into the composite construct of user-experience satisfaction) resulting from users engaging with the different *facets of translated games*. This includes comparing how well localisation products perform after undergoing corrections in response to user feedback, especially in terms of translation-introduced bugs and written language errors (technical and linguistic quality assurance – QA). The GUESS-18 also comes with a dedicated scoring calculator for summarising and visual-ising participant self-reports (Keebler et al. 2020: 55). At the time of writing, the instrument is available in open access.

2.6 Translation Evaluation and Other Target-Specific Experiences

The investigation of reception of VG language-versions can also centre on the translation itself. As Agnieszka Chmiel and Iwona Mazur (2012: 58) observe, 'quality is whatever the customer requires and perceives as good quality', according to the ISO 9000 certificate – a series of standards and best practices 'broadly used for quality assurance in all areas of life'. In VG localisation specifically, Ugo Ellefsen and Miguel Bernal-Merino (2018: 22) postulate that game localisation, on account of the high capacity for personalisation of experiences in VGs, should 'be considered as one aspect of this personalised experience, tailoring the product to fit the specific needs of individuals around the world'. Users can thus be directly asked to self-report about the (indicators of) perceived quality of the translation, or what they disliked about the language transfer or the locale-specific adaptations introduced (and whether or not they even noticed them or how unusual they found them).

Users can even be asked to evaluate the figure of the translator: their diligence in performing their job, whether they appear to be an amateur or a professional, how much money they should be paid for the kind of job they performed, and the like. Similarly, Szarkowska and Gerber-Morón (2018: 9, 19) set out to elicit user preferences and opinions on subtitle-reading experiences as this connected with their conceptualisation of the enjoyment of translation. The way they phrased their questions related to whether participants 'had enough time to read the subtitles, if they re-read subtitles, if they missed words from the subtitles, if they had enough time [...] to follow the on-screen action' and whether or not they perceived 'discrepancies between the spoken dialogues and the text in the [...] subtitles' (Szarkowska & Gerber-Morón 2018: 9, 19). *Facets of user experience* can thus more or less explicitly refer to specific parameters of the target text as investigated by the researchers. Translation-introduced barriers to experiencing a desired, cohesive polysemiotic interaction with a VG may arise at the levels of modalities and beyond them (Bernal-Merino 2020: 299):

- verbal level – for example written errors, non-idiomatic phrasing, poor style, missing translation;
- audio level – for example flat performance by voice talents, culturally inappropriate music,
- visual level – for example inadequate fonts, confusing icons, interfaces, or formatting;
- cultural level – for example breaking taboo, offensive graphics or animations (gestures);

Translation-evaluation *facets of user experience* can correspond to the aforementioned *facets of translated games*. An example would be the investigation of the appropriateness of game experience on a cultural level. As Xiaochun Zhang (2013: 338–339) found, forms of content filtering in social scenarios can be 'surprisingly ubiquitous' and not universally perceived as strictly negative (cf. (*self-)censorship*) – be it for the sake of protection or politeness. This has notoriously been the case with VGs, but also other audiovisual vessels of 'culture, ideology and philosophy'. Researchers might want to tap into this phenomenon with respect to localisation (cf. Zhang 2013), for example investigating whether or not research participants had noticed any content that could be considered distasteful in their (sub)culture; whether they consider such potential inadequacies as disrespectful or acceptable in a VG localisation; to what degree, if at all, they find it necessary for the translators, the local authorities, or the artists behind the source texts to adopt proactive procedures to restrict such content in local language versions, and (more qualitatively) what exact actions they would find appropriate; and if they think the artists behind the game, its translators, or the local authorities should be held accountable if they were to retain the objectionable content.

2.6.1 Dissecting An Example: Communication Mode Research

AVT and MA reception studies can employ questions regarding the user-evaluation of target texts. A study reported by Ramos (2016: 616) asked participants (the 'real target audience' of audio description [AD] – users who need it to experience video materials) to evaluate the language used in AD in terms of functional (in)appropriateness. This study (Ramos 2016) utilised a very similar setup to Ramos (2015; see Section 2.3 on affective responses as *facets of user experience*), however it compared the feelings evoked by different versions of AD (Ramos 2016: 612). The study (Ramos 2016: 615, 616) asked participants with visual impairments if the ADs led them to imagine places, feelings, or actions, on top of asking them to 'rate from 1 to 10 how pleasant or unpleasant the film had appeared to them' and, more open-endedly, what they enjoyed the least/most about the AD version they had experienced – to generate more qualitative comments. These comments on the two versions of the material were then coded onto a matrix based on whether they mentioned quality (e.g. 'Very good'), voice ('I don't like the intonation'), content ('Too much explanation'), or subjectivity ('too neutral') and discussed in relation to the findings from quantitative data (Ramos 2016: 619, 621, 625).

The study (Ramos 2016: 607) compared two version of AD, whereby one aimed for informative objectivity (to build 'a similar experience to that provided by the source texts'), while another was an interpretative 'audio narration' that employed metaphors, connotations, inferences, evaluations, and such like. While this experimental idea can indirectly translate into VG research, it does also inspire ideas of comparing two VG language versions (cf. Section 3 on the *facets of translated games*), resulting from translators employing different strategies – for example those more concerned with conserving source references (cf. *foreignisation*) *vs.* those fully embracing the co-creation (Mangiron & O'Hagan 2006; Bernal-Merino 2016b) of new, (g)local qualities (cf. *domestication*).

Testing the possible effects of these two approaches to game users' experiences could yield very useful insight into both the translation process and translation products. For illustration's sake (other conjectures are equally relevant here), let us say that it could be hypothesised that a degree of foreignisation benefits the perceived educational value of the game, but may instead increase the users' cognitive load indicators – since effective processing of unfamiliar lexis or imagery might require additional mental resources. Likewise, comprehension and emotional response could be hypothesised to be increased through the culturalisation of source-cultural cues and increasing the *illusion of transparency*. And while measuring the overall enjoyment of users and their evaluation of the language version is also enticing, a noteworthy challenge in researching ideas like these naturally would be to even define and reliably operationalise this elusive duality of such concepts (enjoyment–boredom, immersion–emersion, foreign–familiar, etc.) in the first place.

3 Facets of Translated Games

Entertainment software turns the children's game *What if I were ... ?* into actionable virtual reality with no downside. Of course, this is something that continues all the way into adulthood and old age. It may even be that our ever-productive human imagination is utilising the very same neural pathways. After all, advancements in technology allow us to turn into *Homo Ludens* fully (cf. Huizinga 1955). In this context, as Matamala et al. (2020: 130) opine, the current trends in AVT studies are moving 'towards user experience (UX), which aims to elicit the way the user interacts and reacts when exposed to certain stimuli' – in terms of the various aforementioned *facets of user experience* like for example immersion (cf. Section 2). Section 3 overviews the corresponding set of facets of those 'certain stimuli' of which Anna Matamala, Olga Soler-Vilageliu, Gonzalo Iturregui-Gallardo, Anna Jankowska, Jorge-Luis Méndez-Ulrich, and Anna Serrano Ratera (2020: 130) speak.

Research into user response to stimuli can centre on a number of interesting translational phenomena as independent variables. For instance, a research question could ask if foreignisation, domestication, or a mix of both (*facets of translated games*) would be most conducive to some quantified account of what players perceive as emersion or immersion (*facets of user experience*). What we deem *facets of translated games* thus naturally span a large array of features that we will attempt to structure in terms of their granularity – ranging from culture and history, to humour and linguistic variation. Some other formal aspects with potential for academic inquiry include: the choice of font set in each language, the mode of translation (user interface, subtitles, voices, lyrics, sound effects, haptics), and the sociopolitical *constraints* at play in each country at the time of release. Similarly, the unique potential of global multimedia software needs to be tackled, as their complex semio-pragmatic (Bernal-Merino 2016a) virtual world can be programmed differently for each locale.

According to Nimdzi market analysts, game localization services was already a \$330 million business, but there was 'a far larger market for accompanying services such as testing and game audio localization' (Nimdzi 2018). In order to understand how localisation interacts with the market growth and player variety, it is worth looking at the latest player surveys by cross-national entities such as Video Games Europe [VGE] and the European Games Developer Federation [EGDF]. They publish a yearly report (VGE 2022) with the key facts about Europe's VGs sector, according to which there were 126.5 million players in Europe in 2022, 53 per cent of the population aged 6–64 years old plays VGs, 46.7 per cent of European game players are women, and 32 is the average age of a VG player in Europe. The image represented in Figure 1 from said report helps

Figure 1 Infographic from the VGA report of 2022 showing the high percentage of players in Europe in all six age groups: 6–10, 11–14, 15–24, 25–34, 35–44, 45–64. © Video Games Europe.

us realise the widely different profiles, requirements, and expectations of each player group.

Technology companies have inherited audience research practices from the TV and cinema industries and expanded them, utilising the immense flexibility of gaming hardware and software. Almost all digital devices can be turned into a two-way communication system – however basic. This means that, with the right programming, engineers can know how the machine is being used. Such is the case with PCs, smartphones, webpages, TV streaming, game consoles, and gaming portals. Data analytics have been integrated alongside traditional forms of consumer-survey practices – by companies, service providers, governments, etc. – including the logging of users' clicks, search queries, their time spent per screen ... Yet there are differences between the information that can be *mined* – that is uncovered by studying data sets – via raw-data analytics, and with the help of questioners directly working with consumers. While the former can give quantitative information about what a cohort of users have clicked on, the latter can qualify their decisions in a way that supports understanding for better UX design decisions in the future.

For the present research on game localisation, game-user surveys would optimally combine quantitative with qualitative information. Asking feedback from users directly is useful because the issues involved can get rather complex, while also eliciting strong emotional responses that may make users stop interacting with the gaming system (or make them write negative posts about their experiences with it). The tools employed by *GooglePlay*, *Steam*, *Twitch*, and data analytics companies in general, allow them to 'spy' on users and track their behaviour in real-time: what they look at, what they click on, how long they stay playing, whether they stop after failing several times, etc. All this information is useful to game designers, too. From the viewpoint of localisation, it would be useful to know also whether a particular voice was off-putting, or if the humour in a riddle was lost in translation, or if technically incorrect paragraphing (with words bleeding out of dialogue speech-bubbles, cf. *text overflow*) made playing less enjoyable.

The assumption is that everything should work in the same way in each locale as it did in the original language for the original players living in the locale of the developers. When dealing with language, culture, and playability, one must double-check that across all semio-pragmatic nuances (Bernal-Merino 2016a and 2020). We propose to do this, for instance, with a combination of in-game and in-device APIs [Application Programming Interfaces] and player surveys. Alternatively, users can be observed in controlled settings or studied through physiological measurements (e.g. heart rate, eyetracking) and opinion-elicitation in real time (e.g. think-aloud protocol). But let us first briefly explore the complexities we have been referring to (cf. Mejías-Climent 2017: 86–89). Some of the facets we consider most relevant here are: culture, representation, gender, language varieties, humour, poetic forms, accessibility, audio, graphics, locale conventions, gaming platforms, and content restriction. These sub-sections close with a set of possible player-analytical solutions, as well as a discussion on prospects and challenges.

3.1 Handling Culture in Translation

Ideas and products tend to be bound to the group of people that originate them and, by extension, to the culture they inhabit (cf. Sajna 2018: 175). With time, some features may achieve a near-global adoption by other groups of people in other cultures – such as the number zero, chess, sweet and sour chicken, blue jeans, or Superman. But this is not a given – even if the culture of origin may have maintained great influence during its time at the 'summit of history'. One must factor in the multiplying effect of the culture reimagining such creations for their own consumption. In Western cultures, for example, we have enjoyed *Heracles* (from 6th BCE, Greece), *Mulan* (from fourth-century China), and *Sinbad* (from eighth-century Baghdad), which have been recovered several times throughout history in paintings, literature, comics, films, and games. Their latest iterations, highly influenced nowadays by the Hollywood industrial complex, may have lost or gained features to please the mores of the day in the US. People are so used to it that they might not give it a second thought – many around the world would probably feel that they 'know' these characters. For the purpose of non-interactive media largely aimed at passive consumers (readers, listeners, viewers) and in the case of globally shared cultural items (Bernal-Merino 2016b), the characters, locations, and stories feel as lore from other places and times. It is a more intense feeling than a suspension of disbelief, it is a 'foregrounding of belief'; they want that virtual world to be real. For this reason, the filters for historical accuracy and behaviours are relaxed and it is likely that our conceptions share little with those of their creators hundreds of years ago.

Each narrative creates its own logic and, as spectators, we go along for the ride in a state of suspended disbelief. In interactive media, however, rejection may immediately follow if misrepresentations appear, because gameplay relies on (a degree of) agency. In the same fashion, the unique selling point [USP] of VGs is the thrill of becoming, the excitement of role-playing, the joy of generating a simulation users can control within that lore. Indeed, users experience a foregrounding of belief – they want the game fiction to be true. From this viewpoint, games empower players to inhabit an imaginary self in a virtual world where they can engage in any fantasy, from being a racing driver (series like *Formula One*), to a soldier (*Call of Duty* franchise), a teenage girl (*The Last of Us* and *Life is Strange*), a football magnate (*Football Manager* series), or a brain-harvesting alien (*Destroy All Humans!*). Despite the stigma that VGs might still have in some circles, it goes without saying that great ingenuity and large teams are needed to develop these multimedia interactive experiences. Similarly, it takes great creativity to localise them for the enjoyment of people around the world – whatever their language or culture (Bernal-Merino 2018a, 2020).

With time, and thanks to the internet, game genres come closer (Garda 2012), but some features may remain as part of their USP that differentiate them from competitors. VGs in one country may favour graphics, mechanics and stories that are different from those in others. Within the roleplaying genre, there are for example Western RPGs (e.g. game series like *Baldur's Gate*) and JRPGs (e.g. series like *Final Fantasy*). Aside from their origins, the patterns in these two genres, especially in terms of mechanics and plot, can be tricky to pinpoint. Some users may observe that archetypal franchises of Western RPGs hold tendencies toward more mature visual identity and themes influenced by CRPGs (cf. Interplay 1997), TTGs [pen-and-paper, table-top games] (e.g. *Dungeons & Dragons* franchise), and Hollywood. With JRPGs, popular examples may seem to favour the portrayal of younger protagonists and perhaps feature less story branching, while still inheriting concepts and styles from local pop-/sub-cultures (cf. *manhua, manhwa, manga*). Players may be attracted to the creations of their culture – their motifs, design, and intertextual references – because of familiarity, but they may also be intrigued by the exoticism of unknown cultures. Play is make-believe, but if done too rashly in the relationship between two cultures, or if styles are mixed too abruptly, some products will fail in localisation – and not just because of poor linguistic quality (Bernal-Merino 2020). For example, Japanese *Gundam* games have been mostly unappreciated in Western markets because robot stories have been traditionally less popular there. This has changed in the past twenty years (Tighe 2023) – likely thanks in part to the success of the Hasbro/Paramount *Transformers'* series. Another example is US's series *Mortal Kombat* consisting of fighting games enjoying niche appeal in many countries but facing bans in certain territories because of its signature gruesome violence (cf. Mortal Kombat Wiki 2023).

From a business viewpoint – publishers', even more so than developers' – a product that sells well in every country is the desired goal (cf. *globalisation*, *GILT*; O'Hagan 2005). Some games genres excel at this – as player figures show, with franchises like the *Candy Crush Saga* amassing 2.7B downloads in five years (Chau 2018). Their fan numbers are the closest equivalents to those of football, whose sources also count in several billions (FIFA 2023). What might be abstracted from those cases is that the less a game has overt representation of its source culture that could be perceived as preachy, the more likely the wider appeal and thus, success (cf. *glocalisation,* Bernal-Merino 2016b).

3.2 Representation and Player Avatars

Part of the alure of VGs for players is being able to realise an alter ego, whatever the fantasy might be – to design our game-world *avatar.* There has always been a rather wide array of VG protagonists: from spaceships to Pac-Man, Mario to Sonic, Solid Snake to Joanna Dark. Still, the medium has had a bad reputation for portraying what now might be seen as fantasies that are exclusive to the people who used to design, code and play them since the 1970s – heterosexual young male computer geeks. As game markets and industries around the world grew in revenue, matured in sophistication, and diversified in content, competition amongst companies and countries increased, and new sub-genres developed – each focusing on a particular stratum of society. The past decade in particular has seen a rapid surge of VG with female leads such as the popular series of *Horizon* (Guerrilla Games & Firesprite 2017–2023), *The Last of Us* (Naughty Dog 2013-23), *Life is Strange* (Dontnod Entertainment, Deck Nine, Square Enix 2015–2022), and *Control* (Remedy Entertainment 2019) to add to the growing roster begun by Ms. Pac-Man, Samus Aran, Lara Croft, Bayonetta, Commander Shepard, and Faith Connors.

But, with the democratisation of the industry, many users now expect to see even more aspects of their reality (e.g. gender non-binary, body shape, sexual presence, ethnicity) which is made possible in VGs because of their program-mable and customisable nature. Regardless of individual differences, game users have from the beginning had the possibility of experiencing what it is like to be somebody or something else in the world of VGs – allowing them to not just empathically, but *personally* tackle the world from a different perspec-tive. The potential of this in the context of *procedural rhetoric* (cf. Bogost 2011: 11–14, Sterczewski 2012) is illustrated in an interesting set of cases in the genre of Western RPGs. In VGs such as the *Baldur's Gate* series, players *have to* create their own avatars and their choices *will* have a direct impact on the story they live out. The third instalment of *Baldur's Gate* (Larian Studios 2023) has eleven races (human and non-human), twelve classes (or professions), four body types, and gender options for all. While it is standard in the tabletop RPG games [TTRPGs] it was based on, here it is not only an aesthetic choice that is audiovisually represented from beginning to end – these choices are recognised by the game-machine which adapts to them by means of non-playing charac-ters' [NPCs] reactions and changes in storylines. In this way, *Baldur's Gate 3* promises a unique experience for players each time they play – whether they use the same or a different avatar. (For context, one detailed video walkthrough of the main options can be found here Tales of Lumin 2023.)

From the localisation point of view, though, this illustrates why RPGs can be a great challenge, not only because they often have a higher wordcount than a novel, but because translators are obliged to work with *linguistic variables* (Bernal-Merino 2015: 149; Nawrocka 2019; Kabát 2023: 86) to accommodate the variability in character choices and their relationships with NPCs. Linguistic variables are unique to multimedia interactive entertainment software [MIES] which is, at its core, a coded programme. Moreover, each language is unique in the way concepts are articulated (e.g. masculine, feminine, neutral classes), in modes of address/deference (you, you all, your highness . . .), etc.

3.2.1 Gendered Language in Translation

Structural differences between languages can be appreciated in one of the challenges of game localisation, namely the accommodation of morphological and syntactical rules about gendered linguistic items such as nouns, pronouns, articles, etc. (Nawrocka 2019; Kabát 2023: 86). For instance, while English nouns rarely have a morpheme to mark masculine or feminine, some languages, like Spanish do, while others like Polish also use a third, for the neutral gender. This can cause problems – either during game development or its localisation. In *Apex Legends* (Respawn Entertainment 2019) the character of Bloodhound – a masked, mysterious character – was first localised into Polish with the noun and verb forms marked for feminine gender but was changed into non-canonical suffixes for nouns and verbs, e.g. 'Technologiczn*u* Tropiciel*u*', 'Jestem łowc*um* zesłan*um* przez bogów' (Respawn Entertainment 2019). The use of *-u* or *-um* has not been traditionally coded in the Polish language, whose grammar still often necessitates gendered nouns and verbs.

Story-heavy games – particularly RPGs where freedom of character creation and interactions are central – seem to be mostly determined by such challenges, especially when the narrative requires certain utterances to automatically refer to NPCs (AI controlled non-playing characters) that each may have different (or changing) genders. These might be rather complex, far more so than just changing a name coined in a different era (e.g. *Peking* into *Beijing*), or the rules of a basic linguistic algorithm (e.g. in Spanish, if *male*: finish common noun with '*-o*'; if *female*: finish common noun with '*-a*'). As multimedia experiences, interactive entertainment needs to be cohesive across many semiotic layers from linguistic items, to character graphics, world textures, characters' voiceovers, sound effects, lyrics and music, animations, etc. (Bernal-Merino 2016a). This may include the need to address in-game characters (NPCs) correctly, so as to maintain *playability* (Bernal-Merino 2018a, 2016a). There have been titles with transgender and non-binary protagonists where writers employed the inclusive English pronouns, for example in *Desta* (UsTwo 2023) or *Harvestella* (Live Wire 2022). The second case allows the selection of non-binary gender for the played character, as referred to in Figure 2:

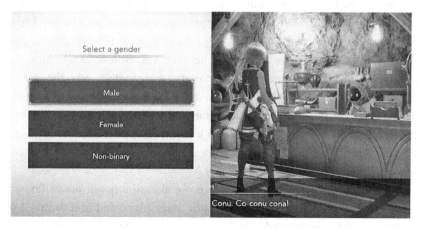

Figure 2 User Interface of video game Harvestella (Live Wire 2022) where players can choose male, female, or non-binary for their playing character [we enlarged the text for accessibility reasons]. © Square Enix

This can also be found in *2064: Read Only Memories* (MidBoss 2015), *Arcadia Fallen* (Galdra Studios 2021), *Starfield* (Bethesda Game Studios 2023). Development and localisation teams also tried their best with their own sets of inclusive pronouns, but the results continue to be problematic and/or inconsistent (Gerblick 2021; Electronic Arts 2022; Arasu 2023). Most accomplished RPGs such as those in the *Baldur's Gate* series have robust character creation options also around sex and gender and they are further supported by very robust localisation pipelines (Adlan 2020), so players seem to be very satisfied with the options after the game patches (Hart 2022). Nonetheless, some fans may see changes as gimmicky and tokenistic, for example if the developers or localisers incorporate features to make the game inclusive, but can in no way change the core vision of the game (Arasu 2023). A deeper analysis can be seen in Tori Schafer's presentation at the 2020 Game Developers Conference in California (Schafer 2020), which provides examples of NPCs having their sex changed (e.g. originally effeminate male characters being changed into female characters) because the local publishers deemed it more acceptable.

3.3 Translating Linguistic Variation

Some gaming communities are so large that they can encompass several countries using the same language or even multiple languages throughout (cf. *code-switching*). That is also why VGs are released trying to satisfy the linguistic needs of communities like the Spanish-speaking gameverse, which nowadays tends to receive a Castilian as well as a Latin-American Spanish version. Chinese is another example, which often has simplified and traditional standards available by default. Perhaps surprisingly, this has so far not been a requirement (not seen on Steam, e.g.) from English players around the world, despite the obvious differences between US, British, South African, Australian, and Indian English (*inter alia*). An example was the game *Scribblenauts* (5th Cell 2009). The main game mechanic [a system of actions available in a game, cf. *ludeme*] in this game is to 'scribble' down words to solve puzzles – so the US developer released a British-English version where e.g. *eggplant* became *aubergine*, *binky* was turned into *dummy*, and *soccer* changed to *football* (Sterling 2009).

While some games employ narrative prose akin to a novel, others favour dialogue presented in the way that comics, stage plays, and film scripts do. Therefore, orality is required, which forces translators to hone into the actual speech in their locales in order to reproduce the freshness that is sought by game creators (Ruskin 2012). This was the case with fantasy sci-fi *Overwatch*

(Blizzard Entertainment 2016), a Multiplayer Online Battle Arena First-person Shooter [MOBA FPS], which features a diverse roster of characters. Some are designed with a real-world backstory, like a very pronounced ethno-cultural background. Each character has a list of expressions that bring to life such origins in the world and voice choices – for example through the Zarya character's Russian accent, Tracer's British English, or Widowmaker's French intensity (PlayOverwatch 2016). This might be why these characters were co-created in parallel for each localised version, as has been reported by Michael Chu from Blizzard in the GDC 2017 talk about Overwatch's 'Thinking Globally' (Chu 2017). Not only that, but the localisation team also needed to write down all character utterances (video sample: GameTec 2022) for the game to display them as captions, as Michael Chu commented later on, even if there is not an established practice of writing down spontaneous street parlance in their language (Forums Blizzard 2022).

Engaging players by maximising the 'cool' factor with contemporary expressions is common in games that want to attract casual players in a light-hearted way. This is particularly routine in Massively Multiplayer Online Games [MMOGs] (e.g. *World of Warcraft* franchise) because of the pull of community competition, and in Multiplayer Online Battle Arena (MOBAs) with global e-sports franchises such as *League of Legends* (Mescon 2011). *Arena of Valor* is a particular example of a game whose popularity seems to be bottlenecked by culturalisation (Sue 2018). All player-versus-player [PvP] games, such as the popular *Fortnite: Battle Royale* (Epic Games 2017) need to achieve and maintain the trendy factor quickly. To do this, they utilise current expressions and references to gaming lore and the wider pop culture. It is part of the lure that may keep players hooked to playing together with the successful implementation of voice-over-IP capabilities to talk with party members during the gaming sessions. These games have specific terminology established by developers, but they also have expressions that appear randomly and are adopted by the whole community. For example, *Fortnite* has the terms such as 'harry pottered' – not covered by the official glossary (Epic Games Dev Community 2023) – which means accidentally getting your in-game avatar stuck in the in-game structures you built (McEvoy 2021).

Localisation teams will endeavour to find similar expressions used by players in each locale. In other cases, translators will suggest new phrases and puns. *Hearthstone* (Blizzard Entertainment 2014) provides countless examples of this, with humour central to the UX of each locale. For instance, one of the cards features a 'Sea Giant'. The English pun on the back of the card takes advantage of the homophony between see/sea (*See? Giant!*). Since a direct translation would not work in most languages, in Spanish, for example, they opted for 'Es la mar de salado [he's salty as the sea]' (see Figure 3), which is a colloquial expression to refer to someone who is pleasant and amusing. It contrasts with the epic look of the characters in the game, but that seems to be the exact light-hearted tone that the developers wanted to set.

3.4 Wordplay, Poetry, Riddles, and Humour

Just like oral traditions and literature have done, some VGs utilise verse and rhyme to bring to life their virtual world ludic propositions. To the prosodic difficulty we have to add the pragmatic dimension of verses (Bernal-Merino 2016a), either because they hold the key to completing the game (like in the various instalments from the *Assassin's Creed* or *Monkey Island* series) or – like in the cases of *Child of Light* (Ubisoft Montreal 2014) and *Tunic* (Isometricorp Games 2022) – because they are even more intrinsically tied to the aesthetics of the proposed game mechanics. Since such lyricism and prosody are essential to the game experience they put forward, VG translators need to exercise their bard skills, and localisation quality assurance testers need to confirm that verse and lexicon choices agree with the playability contributing to the UX as designed. Prosaic or clumsy source-inspired renditions may not only break the foregrounding of belief, but even confuse players, leading them astray and potentially unable to progress the game any further (cf. Bernal-Merino 2016a).

Figure 3 Front and back of the Spanish card for the Sea Giant from the game *Hearthstone* (Blizzard Entertainment 2014) showing the playful translation of the English pun 'See? Giant!' [we enlarged the text for accessibility reasons]. © Blizzard Entertainment.

But such inventiveness is not just the domain of transferring poetic language, ludic wordplay, and riddles that influence gameplay (Bernal-Merino 2020). For example, slapstick humour was very popular during silent cinema (with Charles Chaplin, Buster Keaton, etc.). Now we also find slapstick in for example *Luigi's Mansion* series (Nintendo 2001); situational and dark humour in *Portal 2* (Valve 2007); and adult, physical humour in *Saints Row IV* (Volition 2013). If the intellectual property [IP] is based on known products from literature, television, or comics, the localisation process will follow similar steps seeking to please the existing fandom and avoid problems with copyright authorities. If they are completely new imaginary universes, localisation teams will *transcreate* or *co-create* (Bernal-Merino 2016b) with developers and take advice from publishers – at least under ideal conditions. Players in Europe complained for example that the games under the South Park cartoon franchise had been censored out of some sexual humour that is available in the North American TV cartoon show. This is despite the game having received the maximum rating of PEGI 18. The creators of *South Park: The Stick of Truth* (Obsidian Entertainment 2014) followed the legislation but chose to make several in-game jokes at the expense of European authorities (see: Figure 4) – in line with the UX that they had designed following the spirit of the mutinous TV series.

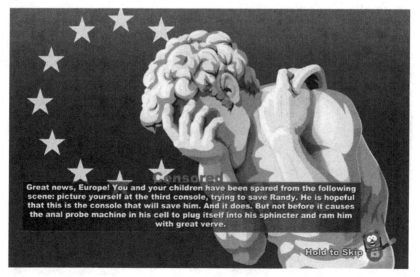

Figure 4 Graphic joke of an embarrassed Michelangelo's David displayed in-game (*South Park: The Stick of Truth* 2014) where the EU banned images about rude sexual humour would appear. © Obsidian Entertainment & South Park Studios.

Similarly, fans of *Ghostwire: Tokyo* (Tango Gameworks 2022) might have noticed the fourth-wall-breaking humour of shop signs (cf. *functions of diegetic on-screen language*; Deckert & Hejduk 2022a) as long as they were familiar with Japanese real restaurant chains, for example that of *Freshmoth Burger* (see: Figure 5), which is a combination of *Freshness Burger* and *Mos Burger* (Ishii 2022).

In other words, the localisation of humour is problematic far beyond the intrinsic textual, culturo-linguistic of audiovisual challenges due to market preferences in each importing locale, age rating regulations, and specialisation of tasks in localisation pipelines (Bernal-Merino 2018a), warranting further research with the help of their userbase.

3.5 Sensory Accessibility

It is often difficult to imagine how other people play for we all judge initially based on how we play ourselves. The spectrum of abilities and preferences is far wider than what any of us can conceive and so it has taken quite long for awareness and technology to catch up with reality to enable all players. UNICEF has recently published a sixty-page toolkit entitled 'Children's rights and online gaming: Industry toolkit on advancing diversity, equity and inclusion' (Unicef 2023) reporting on global key facts and putting forward recommendations for industry decisions makers, politicians, and citizens in general, such as, for example, that 10 per cent of children aged 0–17 in the world live with disabilities (see: Figure 6).

Figure 5 One example of the many intertextual jokes from *Ghostwire: Tokyo* embedded in the graphics that were not localised, losing their humorous function for most game users. © Tango Gameworks.

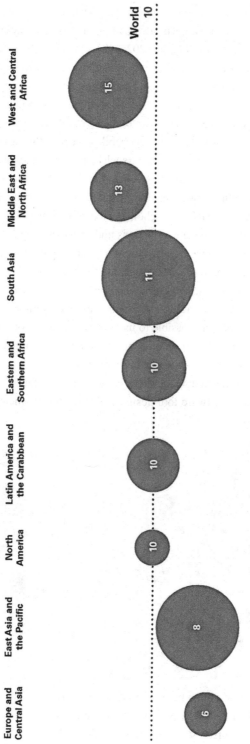

Figure 6 Infographic from UNICEF's report on children's rights and online gaming showing the percentages of disable children in eight world regions. © UNICEF.

Deafness, blindness, paraplegia, or autism are no handicap to use multimedia interactive entertainment software products anymore, as can be evidenced by the photograph in Figure 7 from Xbox (2023).

Notions of personalisation and interactivity are inherent in gaming software and hardware, so the awareness of physical and cognitive accessibility needs has been part of the programme for game consoles and software operating systems for a long time. This is despite its implementation being rather slow and suboptimal, at least up until recently. Nevertheless, accessibility game enthusiast NGOs and academic researchers have helped overcome such historical hurdles in a large part by raising awareness and proposing solutions. Good example of this are the team behind Game Accessibility Guidelines (2023) and the IGDA Game Accessibility Special Interest Group (2023). On the scholarly side, Mangiron (2021) and Greco (2016) offer good practical recommendations and research. Game accessibility highlights the need to combine usability for all and adaptability to all. The one-size-fits-all approach, perhaps understandable at the beginning of the industry, is not only unfair to users, but also bad business in a very competitive mature market and a strategy that would not adhere to the idea of *GILT practices* (O'Hagan 2005) casting as wide a net as possible to incentivise potential consumers. With this in mind, the creators of hardware and software could not continue presuming that all of their clients use their games in the same way.

One of the most significant developments in the industry is the redesign of the actual game engines [a software tool designed for the development of games,

Figure 7 Photograph of young man with severe mobility restrictions enjoying a game with the aid of Xbox © Adaptive Controller™ and Logitech © G Adaptive Gaming Kit™.

Figure 8 Illustrative image from the official PlayStation website showing the three main default presets to help players with special needs adjust their interactivity *The Last of Us: Part II* © Naughty Dog, Playstation.

Figure 9 Alternative game peripherals specially designed to cater for most types of disabilities PlayStation © Access™ Controller, Xbox © Adaptive Controller™, and Logitech© G Adaptive Gaming Kit™ respectively.

such as Unity and Unreal] with enhanced accessibility settings for users. These settings allow users of games developed with said engine to customise the playing experience according to their own (varying) needs, benefiting, at the same time, all other players that simply prefer to tweak the parameters of the game. One excellent example is *The Last of Us: Part II* (Naughty Dog 2020; cf. Santa Monica Studio 2022), which saw its proprietary game engine redesigned to accommodate a detailed array of accessibility options (see: Figure 8) grouped into three main presets: vision, hearing and motor (Sony Interactive Entertainment 2023).

In fact, Playstation (2023), Xbox (2023), and Logitech (2023) (see: Figure 9, ordered respectively) – three of the main game hardware manufacturers – have completed and released their very own set of controllers to enable all players, whatever their needs, leaving Nintendo fans (Dale 2023) in hopeful expectations for the release of the Switch 2 in 2024.

Following the idea that good inclusion design is good game design, such an addition to the core mechanics of the game engines that power the industry has hopefully ushered in a new era in usability, enhancing playability for players with various needs. While accessibility is, strictly speaking, not a linguist task in the traditional sense, it is an inter-semiotic issue, as well as a point of question relating to universal inclusion of users (hence AVT & MA). As such, it constitutes a communication problem between designers, the game-machine, and each player. The reason for this is that MIES establishes and requires a two-way pragma-linguistic conversation with users where the input-output of that conversation – between the game machine and the users – can operate on all layers of semiosis, even those that might not be operable by mono-modal media (Bernal-Merino 2016a), in accordance with the abstraction: GAME-MACHINE ↔ MESSAGE LAYER (8) ↔ SIGN (24) ↔ PLAYER. Translators, linguists, editors, proof-readers, and LQA testers bridge such gaps between creators and consumers for each locale. Sensory accessibility can thus be considered both in terms of *facets of game users* as well as *facets of translated games* since it can be variably realised depending on the requirements and legislation of each importing locale – an issue to be explored further.

3.6 Voice, Music, Sound Effects Localisation

While text has always been at the core of localisation, voices (actors' performances and regional mannerisms and accents) can make or break a game experience (Maxwell-Chandler & O'Malley-Deming 2012). The human voice carries myriad information in its inflexion that users cannot but have an emotional, instinctive reaction to when they hear it. Case in point, many cinephiles tend to dislike dubbed films, opting to watch them in the original versions with subtitles, or even ignoring them completely if English is not the main language. This is even more so the case with interactive media, for these products require the direct input from players to progress (Ellefsen & Bernal-Merino 2018).

Music can be used in VGs to create soundscapes that bring to life the virtual experience put forward by the game. For example, a game where players can live out a Caribbean pirate fantasy could feature original sea shanties throughout the sailing episodes, mirroring the real behaviour of sailors during seafaring times. If these songs were changed, it could break the intended realistic historical tone centred around these themes. However, songs and lyrics may be utilised as part of the storytelling or the inner thoughts of a character and, in those cases, it might be worth localising to maintain the UX. *Final Fantasy XVI* (Square Enix 2023), for one, has a song entitled 'Moongazing' which is sung in Japanese by J-pop hitmaker Tsuki Wo Miteita (male voice) in the original version, while the US version has LA vocalist Amanda Achen (female voice) performing a similar but different song, entitled 'My Star'. Game designers needed the heartfelt lyrics at the end of the game to touch players emotionally and so decided to rearrange the song and call upon an American singer popular for her lyrical contribution at Disney.

A more localisation-intensive effort was carried out by Polish developer/ publisher CD Projekt for *The Witcher 3: Wild Hunt* (2015) where all songs were translated and performed in seven languages (English, French, German, Polish, Portuguese, Japanese, and Russian). A multilingual variant of 'The Wolven Storm (Priscilla's Song)' which remixes all localisations into one song can be accessed on YouTube (The Witcher 2015). Similarly, in the *Nier* game series, there are some differences in the soundscape players immerse themselves into, as the original (Morin 2021) Japanese *Nier Replicant* (Cavia 2010a) has a more ethereal sound, while the global version *Nier Gestalt* (Cavia 2010b) seems designed to be edgier. Games based on big-screen franchises often need to reuse the voice talent to attract players (Mejías-Climent 2021), but this may be legally impossible or not viable financially for all locales. As a result, players may criticise the game, even if everything else is of an acceptable standard. Publications on game audio localisation are still scarce and often rather technical for they change the entire sound design of the game and are delivered by the engineers that work with them in studio (Crosignani 2011; Shibayama & Taniyama 2012).

For multimedia, including VGs, audio assets can be the most suggestive element of a playing experience. Horror games have intricate and distressing scores to immerse players in desperate survival situations. These special effects can sometimes be toned down or changed during localisation because, for a particular locale, they might not mean what was intended in the source. This includes situations in which soundtracks may elicit culturally unacceptable ideas, such as in cases with screams of despair and moans of sexual pleasure. Music will also be changed if the lyrics are deemed offensive, and if the melody seems to plagiarise copyrighted albums or appears sacrilegious in a religious community.

3.7 Transferring Visual Information

Despite VGs being multimodal, the way in which their visuals (symbols, icons, animated textures, texts like diegetic *on-screen language*) are implemented to enhance functional (in-game pragmatics, Bernal-Merino 2016a; cf. Deckert & Hejduk 2022a) information may often receive more designer attention than other game assets, following the mantra that humans are visual creatures. The translation of images in picture books and comics has received some attention within Translation Studies research with the research of for example O'Sullivan (1999) and Zanettin (2008). Many games need to represent worn cityscapes and lived locations, which require writers and graphic designers to populate such virtual places with real-world items or imagined ones, but which are at the same time recognisable by players, therefore contributing to the playing experience (Barnes 2012). As an illustration, in a presentation at the 2012 Localization Summit by a localisation manager William Barnes at Blizzard Entertainment, we learn the company vision was as follows: 'Make the game feel like it was designed for any player that sits down in front of it, regardless of their locale' (Barnes 2012).

Visual information can be culturally bound for it may have a meaning specific to the people that produces it that can differ from the meaning assigned to it by people in other countries. For example, the *Buzz* quiz-show franchise's questions and visual cues may have to be created from scratch for each locale, so that American pop-TV questions do not appear to Italian or Chinese players (Crosignani & Ravetto 2011). Fictional worlds are not much different. The science-fiction game series *StarCraft* localised all the graphic assets that decorated the playing fields for its 2010 second instalment (see: Figure 10), even if these were, strictly speaking, not functionally necessary (cf. *optionality of on-screen language*, Deckert & Hejduk 2022a: 71). It was a wink and a nod to players outside of the US that they were being taken into account and catered for and the creators were happy with how they came out (Barnes 2012). These details may help player-immersion and, ultimately, brand loyalty (Bernal-Merino 2018b; Deckert & Hejduk 2022a). Figure 10 shows one of the billboard examples (with English, Russian, and Korean) mentioned by Barnes (2012) regarding his work on the localisation of *StarCraft II: Wings of Liberty* (Blizzard Entertainment 2010) for the global market.

In contrast, the *Metro* franchise is set in Russia, and the *Yakuza* series in Japan. The graphics in these two games favour realistic buildings with the signs (in Russian and Japanese, respectively), supporting the verisimilitude of the game world, since it would be realistic in these places to display native

Figure 10 Billboard by army barracks saying 'The Dominion keeps you Safe' with a graffiti saying 'Hey, Mengx' localised textually and graphically into Russian and Korean respectively. © Blizzard Entertainment, William Barnes.

languages. In these cases, graphics can be captioned (Deckert & Hejduk 2022a). These rules also apply to icons in the UI (menus), symbols wrapping around game geometry (bitmap textures) and, of course, characters.

Characters may be redesigned as older, as is the case with some Japanese games coming to Western countries. As described by *The Gamer* source (Morin 2021), one such example is *Nier Gestalt* (Cavia 2010b), whose playable character was changed to be the father, rather than an adolescent brother of titular Nier. The source also clarifies that *Nier Replicant* (Cavia 2010a) was 'technically the original version of the game' before the creation of the Western release, as the publisher wagered that 'the sales abroad would be lackluster' without these changes. This also necessitated some other changes, for example in the VG packaging and cover art (see Figure 11).

3.8 Locale versus Device Considerations

One of the most difficult tasks game localisation managers (Bernal-Merino 2016b) have to deal with is to decide 'what' to translate and for 'which' platforms before deciding 'how' to translate (Bartelt-Krantz 2017; Maxwell-Chandler & O'Malley-Deming 2012; Deckert 2021). As consumers, we are rarely aware of the many ports a game may have – all of which have to be play-tested separately in-device by functionality and linguistic testers. The official website of TestronicLab (2023) – a company fully dedicated to functionality, localisation and compatibility testing – gives a good overview of what VGs need. The old chasms amongst devices have narrowed considerably and now

Figure 11 Adolescent avatar for the Japanese release and a mature, rugged one for Western regions from the game *Nier*. © Square Enix.

most developers strive for a multi-platform global distribution. For example, *Life Is Strange: True Colors* (Deck Nine 2021) was released on Windows, Windows Apps, PlayStation 4, Xbox One, Xbox Series X/S, Stadia, PlayStation 5, Nintendo Switch. The difference in image quality is the most obvious one to players, as can be appreciated in the comparison in Figure 12, but the consequences of playing in lower resolution do affect UI and captions. Porting can lead to changes in localisation because of the constraints on memory for multimedia assets. Employing a less capable hardware forces companies to reduce graphics, texture, and shadow complexity, and platform usability compliance means that controllers need to be remapped, recalibrated, and replaced in game code and pop-ups [contextual menus].

Each gaming platform may have different requirements regarding the type of content they allow (based on the expectations of their main user-base) and the legal framework of each locale they provide entertainment to. For example, the aforementioned *Life is Strange* instalment (Deck Nine 2021) was rated *M* [17+] by the ESRB in the US (2023) but 12 by the USK in Germany (2023). When all such constraints are considered in the decision-making of localisation managers, it is easier to understand why and how the same game title can have different implementations depending on the locale and the platform. While it may seem shocking and some players may jump to conclusions based on the censorship that was carried out in the bygone eras, it is in fact quite common that

Figure 12 PS5 rich graphics compared with Nintendo Switch which, having less capable hardware, has to reduce polygons, texture resolution and visual effects. © Square Enix PlayStation, Nintendo, respectively.

entertainment media (and all products for that matter) are slightly tweaked to facilitate penetration in new markets to woo new consumers (McLaughlin & Muñoz-Basols 2021).

While in many cases of translatorial decision-making, the object under consideration is a given, a more 'elementary' phase in other cases would be to first detect the assortment of components to be transferred (Deckert 2021: 99). Some levels of localisation depth to consider include: *box'n'docs* only (just packaging and user manuals), the website (e-store page), user interface (menus), captions (subtitles and messages), voiceover (audio-only files), textures (visually representing words or cultural images), animations (culturally bound movements), lip-synched videos (in-game cinematic sequences), characters and storylines (unknown or upsetting to some locales), haptics (vibration of game controller), proprioception and equilibrioception (i.e. are intense VR/AR experiences favoured or as yet unadopted?).

All things considered, there remains the problem of maintaining sufficient quality across all supported devices (console, PC, phone), regardless of their characteristics like monitor size, processing power, or type of user input (Bernal-Merino 2020). This may also compromise satisfaction with a given translation mode, so aspects like subtitle font size may need to be tweaked on mobile phone releases compared to consoles that are typically hooked up to computer or television sets (Impey 2018). Figure 13 illustrates an example of the two UIs from the PC and mobile versions (respectively) of *Hearthstone* (Blizzard Entertainment 2014).

3.9 Genre, Motifs, Local Gaming Conventions

Although VGs started in the USA, quickly followed by Japan, entertainment software is now a multibillion industry in most countries – the leading ones being China, South Korea, Germany, the United Kingdom, France, and Canada. NewZoo market analysis (Wijman 2023) estimates that the global game revenue is already at $184Bn, 49 per cent of which is generated on mobile devices (see: Figure 14). Not only is the gaming landscape changing from desktops to portables, but the North American market is now only 27 per cent of the total. The consumer growth of the past twenty years has mostly happened in countries that have relied on quality localisation (Bernal-Merino 2020) for they don't have English as their mother tongue. It could be said that there is a global(-ish) game culture thanks to the fact that interactive entertainment has developed hand-in-hand with digital technology and the Internet. It is a young industry when compared to television (approx. 100 y. o.), cinema (approx. 120 y. o.), recorded music (approx. 140 y. o.), printed books (approx. 330 y. o.) (Freeman & Rampazzo 2018; Rauscher et al. 2021).

Figure 13 Computer and mobile UIs of *Hearthstone*. © Blizzard Entertainment.

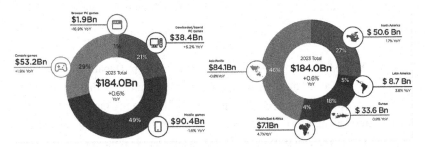

Figure 14 Infographics showing the amount of money generated in each
gaming device type, and the main world regions. © Newzoo.

Anthropologically speaking, genres can be said to be falling within similar
boxes, but motifs and conventions vary in their timing depending on each
medium, country, and their history. This is what professional localisation
teams evaluate to avoid succumbing to the 'literal translation' fallacy – well-
intended, but often based on poor source text understanding or resulting in
inadequate target text wordsmithing and penmanship (Bernal-Merino 2015:
55). Operations like direct, word-for-word translation may impose source-text

lexicon, syntax, and style onto the target text, and they may turn out to be linked with poor quality claques. Investigating this empirically in game translations seems a worthy effort, then. While languages have always influenced each other, it should be noted that the speed of change accelerated due to factors like globalisation and Internet technologies – as revealed by 55 per cent of the Internet traffic being in English, despite only around 16 per cent of the world's population having it as a mother tongue (Internet Society Foundation 2023).

When it comes to studying genres, TechHQ report that Western players show a preference for shooters and football managers, while Eastern players favour battle royale and MOBA genres (Zulhusni 2023). There is a movement towards convergence in gaming which benefits companies, similar to past tendencies in television, cinema, comic books, and literature. Nonetheless, the identities of players and representation continue to be at the core of games, leading developers to *glocalise* their design and enable their employees to co-create their content for the benefit of all (Bernal-Merino 2016b, 2018b). Investigating the reception of this should likewise follow suit.

3.10 Censorship, Self-censorship, and Taboo

Regulations imposed by lawmakers and opinion-makers begin as industries grow and start having a significant impact on citizens, public opinion, and tax revenues (cf. Zhang 2013). Overt censorship is clearer when games are based on or portray real historical events, as in war and strategy games, or world-base adventure games (Mandiberg 2018). But it does also happen with fantasy, science fiction, and social simulation games, because people can perceive representational and behavioural patterns reminiscent of the real-world ideas underneath the veneer of a game.

While some games might be banned and later modified and re-released, allowing for their commercialisation, others are self-censored for specific locales by their creators trying to be sensitive to cultural and historical reasons, as in the case of the Japanese version of *Fallout 3* (Bethesda Game Studios 2008) a post-apocalyptic RPG which was modified in the gameplay fragment where there is an option of nuking Megaton – an important city. The option was removed (cf. *auto/self-censoring*) due to Japan's nuclear history with the USA, to minimise potential offence. The same game was not released in India, due to 'unspecified content that Microsoft believes could offend consumers' (Lee 2008) – likely due to being able to hunt and sell two-headed mutated cows which look very similar to sacred Brahman cows. Another case is one of the instalments of the British *The Sims* being pulled from mobile e-stores in China, Saudi Arabia, UAE, Oman, Kuwait, Qatar, Egypt (cf. Radulovic 2018). Similar manipulations take place in other countries, with examples from game series like the Scottish *Grand Theft Auto* due to violence and sexual innuendos, the Japanese *Valkyrie Drive* series because of nudity, and the US *Mortal Kombat*, whose titles faced bans because of mechanics that on the diegetic level are explicitly sadistic, but that players have to follow on the game-rules level in order to win (cf. Mortal Kombat Wiki 2023). It should be pointed out that researchers may investigate how audiences reflect on these changes made to local versions.

Changes like these can furthermore be found in content for the same locale but for a different strata of players. *Assassin's Creed Origins* (Ubisoft 2017) released a *Tour Mode* designed specifically for children who wanted to explore the main classic Greek metropolis and cities without the killing mechanic the game franchise is known for. In contrast to its apparent educational purpose, however, the game mode misrepresented local sculptures by censoring them with shells (see: left-side Figure 15). While this might have been done to avoid controversy with parents, schools, and politicians, it instead incentivised backlash from fans – as ridiculed by *Kotaku International*: 'In a striking departure from history, Assassin's Creed: Origins' Discovery Tour mode

Figure 15 Cropped screenshots from *Assassin's Creed Origins* (left, © Ubisoft) censored classic Greek statues with shells, and *The Witcher 3: Wild Hunt* (right, © CD Projekt) censored graphics by painting clothes on nude character textures.

replaces any nipples or genitalia with seashells. There was no nudity in Ancient Egypt, it appears'. (Kotaku 2018). Another case, *The Witcher 3: Wild Hunt* (CD Projekt Red 2015), is an example of content adaptation during localisation of the core game, due to visual content deemed too explicit. In this action-RPG for mature players, based on an internationally known Polish book series (Sapkowski 1990), there are several romantic encounters where sexual intercourse may be initiated. However, in Japan and the Middle-East, graphics were retextured as clothed so that there would be no nudity (see: right-side Figure 15), in contrast with the Western version and the spirit of the novels written by Andrzej Sapkowski (1990).

3.11 Possible User-Centred Localisation Solutions

We start from the idea that all the aforementioned *facets of translated games* imply decision-making – for instance as to whether to domesticate or foreignise, whether to standardise a character's dialect or attempt to render it using another locale-related variety, what font to use for in-game text. The effects of the decisions made need to be captured scientifically. For instance, as we talk about the need to understand the relationship between domestication-foreignisation and immersion as a *facet of user experience*, we can use available Likert-type scales and psychometric questionnaires developed to examine this facet empirically. In doing so, we address the benefits of obtaining numerical reception data, but at the same time point to some methodological caveats of self-reports as well as the challenges of research that involves players interacting with games in experiments and/or providing their input.

Application Programming Interfaces (APIs) are small applications that can run in the background of any other programmes. All digital devices nowadays can have several APIs running at any given time even without users logging on with their credentials. Game consoles, mobile phones, and gaming platforms all have these APIs collecting large amounts of data. Our new line of player research can have APIs generated for specific purposes with localisation quality in mind, to collect meaningful sample sizes. They can be cross-referenced with after-play qualitative surveys. Since in VGs less conventional sign layers sometimes need to be localised – for example, proprioception, equilibrioception, touch, graphic textures, sounds, music (Bernal-Merino 2016a and 2020) – one productive outcome relates to testing this aspect of the translational framework.

Indeed, basic APIs are already employed by localisation managers, but they focus only on basic issues such as 'has this string been translated' or 'does the voice-over/dubbing file have a different quality'. This implies that purpose-made APIs for the aforementioned *facets of translated games* might not be problematic to implement into the workflows. This would however mean that, although some queries can be generalised to many games, most would need to be specific to each genre and, at times, unique to the game, because of the specific vision of UX being put forward by designers. The future is likely to present further prospects and challenges. It is clear that VGs will continue exploring the possibilities of interactive media and that more experiences will arise from the integration of better haptic technology in VR [virtual reality], XR/ER [extended reality], and AR [augmented reality]. Our conjecture is that translation-related challenges will persist and increase in complexity as experiences get closer to real life.

Media products in general, and VGs in particular, are very often brushed aside as unimportant, time-wasting hobbies of little particular value. Yet, from literature to films, comics to sculptures, and tapestries to VGs, creative products are as much an inherent result of human DNA as leukocytes, hormones, or emotions. Storytelling media can be seen as channelling the need for meaning that pervades other activities as well. A sense of community and civilisations can only be built on the basis of stories, so all human groups develop artefacts to remind themselves of their leitmotivs: the collection of icons, values, characters, and behaviours that are socially applauded. Minor variations may be acceptable, but VGs, as showcased by the ludo-narrative discussion, may be a unique technological form of participation in this process, rather than just a form of reusing previously discovered semiotic channels (Bernal-Merino 2016a). Even if VG culture becomes more homogenised worldwide, differences may remain because of natural protectionism in cultures, language preservation, workflow practicalities, and politics. In this sense, it is useful to compare many entertainment industries (cinema, television, music, comics, etc.) and their endless journeys towards some kind of convergence thanks to global communication. Artistic modes of expression have been enjoyed and reimagined throughout history, while each nation retains its uniqueness. Table-top RPGs and software computer RPGs may borrow from each other, but they remain different.

Thus, one more closing *facet of translated games* to be considered in the future localisation-reception research is whether or not game translation is even attempted in the first place, for certain genres and locales. This is an issue relevant for minority language users as well as for majority languages that are not yet profitable markets, which was the case with Brazilian Portuguese only a few years ago (Harkin 2023). Maria Koscelníková (2021: 1) found that Slovak 'struggles to maintain a presence in the video game industry', reporting a similar case for Serbian, Croatian, and Slovenian. Comparably, Itziar Zorrakin-Goikoetxea's (2023: 139) reception study in Spain sheds light on the preferences of Basque and Catalan users, finding that 'localisations into minority languages would be welcomed by players', inviting more comprehensive studies 'that address this sociolinguistic aspect of video game localisation'. Future research can therefore compare more specific experiential factors of language users stimulated with source versus target locale versions.

4 Facets of Game User(s)

Ultimately, researchers investigating localisation reception need to assume that different characteristics of individuals (e.g. personalities, preferences, backgrounds, and language proficiency levels) can influence the relationship between a language version of a VG and how it is received by users. Therefore, a third and complementary set of facets we map out in this Element concerns game users at a different level to that of *facets of user experience* (cf. Section 2) or *facets of translated games* (cf. Section 3) – the two other critical components of the blueprint we wish to propose. Compared to the *experience facets* (e.g. how fun a given game appears) – *users facets* can be thought of as more stable across time (e.g. which games a studied person likes). This reflects our assumption that findings regarding localisation reception will heavily depend on the individual differences found between the studied subjects. In other words, *user facets* are individual characteristics that can be taken as given before the start of the study. By contrast, *experience facets* are experiential constructs which tend[4] to be more contextual, for example relying on first being directly induced through user stimulation by some VG material. This is why *users facets*, in terms of experimental design, can conversely function as more stable indicators already present in subjects (e.g. control variables, sources of potential covariance with dependent variables, or independent variables in between-group designs).

By isolating *facets of game users* we wish to argue that there is a need for greater scholarly understanding of who study participants are and how they differ. A key premise to be recognised is that it is over-reductive to conceptualise game users as a homogenous group. One point here is that the label of *users* can be conceptualised to cover different modes of translated VG consumption, rather than just VG playing. If *users* are conceptualised as, more literally, *those who use VGs*, then they might not just be conceptualised as players, but also game viewers, creators, and other figures relevant for the phenomenon, both sociologically and industry-wise. These figures may even denote the same one person – generally

---

[4] A noteworthy degree of overlap and construct interrelatedness between those two sets of facets cannot be overstated. It should be assumed for instance that repeated experiencing of a VG title/ genre/translation would likely contribute to or shape that user's overall *preferences* (users facet).

referring to those who use a range of VGs for their individual variety of use cases. This terminological point should be further investigated in and of itself.

In parallel, users vary along a range of interrelated dimensions that further play a role in how they experience translated games, some of the most relevant ones being user needs (e.g. in terms of sensory, motor, cognitive accessibility), personality and individual differences, knowledge and experience, preferences as well as sources of playing motivation. These tentative compartments are not autonomous of one another, with some categories being broader and more influential than others. For example, an individual's personality traits will underlie some of the other *facets*, and a user's background assumptions and prior experience will shape their preferences and motivate them variably.

4.1 Media Accessibility Needs

Users vary in how they access games, and games are either designed or adapted to be experienced more fully across multiple dimensions which go beyond language, which is central in this volume – especially considering the wealth of academic achievements and industry resources that are available on gaming accessibility. Some of the options available for access provision when it comes to vision compensation – as just one subset of cases – are colour filers or colour customisation, binaural audio (Neidhardt & Rüppel 2012), sonification (Ribeiro et al. 2012), that is 'the use of non-speech audio to convey information or perceptualize data' (Khaliq & Dela Torre 2019: 146) as well as haptic feedback transmitted via gloves (Yuan & Folmer 2008) or tongue display units (Chebat et al. 2011). In a similar vein, guidelines and resources have been developed to enhance VG accessibility (*AbleGamers.org, GameAccessibilityGuidelines.com, SpecialEffect.org.uk, CanIPlayThat.com*, Xbox Accessibility Guidelines, and many more). These are frequently made by users or in consultancy with them, to isolate a number of dimensions – for example motor ability, cognition, vision, hearing, and speech. Remarkably, establishing to which extent or in what form users are consulted for these may constitute a starting point for thinking about their engagement.

Returning to linguistically mediated access, a prominent case of intralingual transfer is what we can broadly refer to as 'easy-to-understand'[5] language (E2 U) – 'an umbrella term used to cover specific and established forms of language comprehension enhancement' (Perego 2020: 17). While some work has been done on E2 U and subtitling that relied on reception data (Bernabé-Caro et al. 2020; Oncins et al. 2020; Matamala 2021), the application of E2 U

---

[5] While the label serves our purpose, Matamala (2022: 130) talks about 'a wide array of terms that are used to refer to concepts related to E2U language: Easy-to-Read, Easy Reading, Easy Read, Easy Language, Plain Language, Simple Language, Simplified Language, Citizen Language, and Clear Writing, among others.

language for VG translation remains to be examined, critically with input from users. Matamala's (2022: 140–141) observation is highly relevant here. She points out that 'It remains to be seen how E2 U language will be integrated into different formats and products. It remains to be seen what the role of the user will be when developing accessible content and how the user will be defined, probably moving beyond the realm of disability into a capability-based model'.

Scholars should also consider what their subject is capable of in terms of particular equipment, especially in remote-protocol studies. That would include:

- whether a particular VG stimulus would be cognitively appropriate for their subjects' profile and what is being studied (e.g. a suitable degree of puzzle difficulty for children).
- if their subjects would be proficient enough or otherwise able to engage with a particular VG material (e.g. a competitive multiplayer first-person shooter for first-time players).
- how confident one should be in the user's ability to operate a computer to a degree that would allow them to run the VG stimulus material (e.g. while running a remote online study where participants are supposed to download and install a VG on their machine).
- what kind of hardware is available for participants and if their hardware would be compatible with the prepared VG stimulus material (e.g. studying console players).

Of course, user needs might influence their preferences for certain modes (e.g. AD, SDH) and devices (e.g. hardware with bigger screens) that ought to be accommodated or otherwise considered at an early stage of planning a study.

4.2 Personality, Individual Differences, and Background

One challenge of undertaking game translation user research (GTUR) is investigating the results through the prism of players as individuals – 'the playing practices of old as well as young people, both women and men, those who are eager and dedicated gamers as well as those who are not' (Kallio et al. 2011: 328). General parameters to be considered are demographic data like age, gender, orientation, and identity (Bernal-Merino 2018b), but also the participant's socio-economic status, income, or interest in a game's source culture, which might influence how they experience it. Some examples of particular topics to be discussed with participants (e.g. in semi-structured interviews, surveys, focus groups) might include issues like:

- the importance that users place on localisation while deciding to buy a VG title, for example whether or not they go out of their way (e.g. frequenting news sources) to assess the quality of localisation (Bernal-Merino 2020) before purchasing their product,

- whether they typically play games that are similar to the historical/sociocultural contexts they are familiar with, or those set in distant cultures (if they have a preference like that at all),
- how likely they would be to set the diegetic language (e.g. voice acting, on-screen language) to one that relates to the cultural context of the game (e.g. Polish in *The Witcher*, Russian in the *Metro*, American English in *Tom Clancy's The Division* game series)
- what would be the purpose of the above – for immersion, or to have a feeling of what it might be like to play the game in that locale, or as a way to contact or educate oneself about a foreign language or culture?
- are viewers inclined to engage with the *fictional*[6] dimensions of VGs (e.g. metaphors, plot, setting, aura, meaningful linguistic content, the implied player's profile) or do they mostly pursue the *ludic* dimension of the medium that enables emergent and immediate gameplay (e.g. simulation systems, rules, and what performative actions they allow the player to take).

Participants might also differ in terms of their immersive tendencies (Witmer & Singer 1998), and possibly in their proclivity to experience other constructs like humour or enjoy VG challenges. Perhaps the most psychologically intuitive way in which users might be dissimilar is in their personalities. One kind of widely accepted measure of this that researchers can implement in their studies of game translation user research is an abbreviated inventory (some are just several self-descriptive statements long) for the CANOE/OCEAN model – better known as The Big Five. The model 'identifies personality as a combination of interpersonal skills, attitudes, motivations, emotional and experimental styles' and consists of five personality factors in openness, conscientiousness, extraversion, agreeableness, and neuroticism – determining each person's personality domains as 'the likeliness of each dimension' with either high or low inclinations (Peever et al. 2012: 1). As a practical illustration, Johnson, Wyeth, Sweetser, and Gardner (2012: 2) investigated the correlations between personality and six subscales of experience ('competence, sensory and imaginative immersion, flow, tension/annoyance, challenge, enjoyment') in 466 respondents, mostly university students. Notably, participants were primed via

---

[6] For an overview of the ludic–narrative dimensions of VGs, cf. Prajzner (2019: 22–23). The general idea is that while game rules are essential to VGs as a medium, whatever they semantically represent (diegetically or symbolically) is subjective and 'optional'. Although relevant, the historical disagreements in game studies about the nature of the tension between these two dimensions (cf. Pearce 2005) might lead some to object to reducing the artistic and multimodal VG texts to just win condition systems.

a guided recall process to describe in detail 'what was happening when they were most recently playing their current favourite game'; they had a chance to win a prize to incentivise a large pool of responses (Johnson et al. 2012: 3). A different study by Peever, Johnson, and Gardner (2012: 1, 3) was conducted to 'ascertain whether people with certain personality types exhibit preferences for particular game genres'. The study identified some statistically significant links, for example that 'people who enjoy casual, music and party games tend to be more extraverted and that people who enjoy role-playing games, [...] and real-time strategy games tend to be less extraverted'. Conceding the model of pursuing reliability and candidness in science, researchers too should be aware of their demographic profiles, because it is not impossible that even trained experts (unconsciously) phrase or discuss results in a way that covertly represents specific points of view, their general tendencies, or other perspectives stemming from their background.

4.3 Knowledge, Experiences, Attitudes, and Preferences

One of the most important criteria for researchers of translation reception is the linguacultural profile and encyclopaedical knowledge of their users, to the point where it might not be enough to let participants self-report that they speak certain languages. While 'it may be widely believed that biographical reports and self-rated proficiency scores are sufficient to [reliably] capture differences in language aptitude', there are tools to test users in terms of their general language proficiency instead (Lemhöfer & Broersma 2011: 326). One test is a quick and easy-to-use vocabulary-knowledge predictor presented in a semi-gamified form of a yes-no exam that scores between 0 and 100 per cent (e.g. LexTale.com). Depending on the phenomenon studied, participants scoring below or above a certain threshold may be included in the study (or conversely excluded from it), but their scores can also become potential correlates (covariates) in statistical modelling.

In principle, researchers should control for variables like participants' expertise in VGs (have they played the specific stimulus material? Have they played similar titles? Have they played other titles from the same genre?), their professional background (e.g. have they translated games? Do they know how games are translated?), culture (have they any knowledge about the historical or cultural context of events presented in the experienced material?), audiovisual literariness (what other VGs have they played? What other directly relevant audiovisual media and modes of translation could they have encountered?), affiliation with specific game-related views and gaming subcultures (are there any preconceived notions that could have been consequential for their reading of the VG? Do they identify as gamers, non-gamers, or neither?), or intensity of participation (how many hours per week do they use VGs directly, indirectly, with or without friends, etc.) Prejudices or valent attitudes towards users' relation with other game users, VGs in general or specific genres, particular titles, or game producers might be deconstructed in a post-task interview, as long as the researcher provides space for the participant to be able to safely open up about them. Some specific questions for players might investigate the following issues:

- to what extent localisation bugs and translation errors impact their experience – how they would weigh for example uninspired dubbing, poor subtitling, incorrect use of variables, text overflow, character misattribution (Kabát 2023: 86–89) confusing UI labels, inadequate font size or colour on a scale from inconsequential to egregious.
- which content-changes they consider necessary in their particular territory – ranging from graphics, animations, characterisation, storylines, music, sound effects, historical context, political data, ideological belief systems, names, textures, UI, symbols, taboo, etc.
- what is the percentage of players willing to stop playing a game due to low perceived quality of localisation – ranging from voices, captions, UI, or cultural offense – and whether or not they reverted to the source language after quitting the localised version (Bernal-Merino 2020).
- which kinds of legislation influence translation in particular territories and to what degree players therein are aware of that and/or support it.

It should also be noted that study participants may come to experience the VG material with more or less positive or negative states of mind, which needs to be controlled for by the researchers, as it could (re)shape how they experience a game. Scheduling pre-task meditative practices and questions that allow participant responses about their current mood are in order.

4.4 Sources of Playing Motivation

Not unexpectedly, reasons for experiencing VGs ultimately constitute a summary of many of the aforementioned *facets of user experience*. Wiemeyer et al. review a selection of psychological models of PX incorporating factors that may contribute to the subjective reception of a VG, including the users' motivation to play (2016: 248–250). It is claimed that intrinsic motivation to engage with VGs may develop from play potentially fulfilling certain basic needs of users (cf. *self-determination theory*), which include: the need for competence ('being able to meet the requirements of tasks'), need for autonomy (freedom to select own goals, 'evaluating the causes of success or failure'), and need for relatedness (social interactions, belonging to a community). These patterns however can be extended (cf. *PENS – Player Experience of Need Satisfaction*) to encompass the fulfilment of needs for presence (including three subdimensions of presence: physical, emotional, narrative), and control (usability, intuitive navigation of the game). It has also been reported that intrinsic motivation may be maintained by the attraction of users' focus (cf. attention distribution), users' recognition of play as meaningful or relevant, users' confidence that sufficient engagement will result in success, and users' sense of reward or satisfaction with their accomplishments (*cf. ARCS strategies*). Being intrinsically motivated can be further characterised by states typically associated with heightened levels of personally gratifying involvement (cf. e.g. flow; Csikszentmihalyi 1990): decreased self-consciousness, time distortion or transformation, clarity of game objectives, looping in immediate and easily comprehensible feedback, and a sense of prowess (Wiemeyer et al. 2016: 250). Wiemeyer et al. further refer to the study by Takatalo et al. (2010), who propose ten subdimensions of PX in their *Presence-Involvement-Flow Framework*. Sub-experiences of play incorporated into the aforementioned Takatalo et al. (2010)'s framework include: satisfying curiosity, exploring the story, and dramatisation (Wiemeyer et al. 2016: 251). Emotional responses (negative and positive, possibly including humour, entertainment, and more) as well as playing time were also mentioned in the literature overview as parts of PX (Wiemeyer et al. 2016: 251–252). Certain integrative models of PX were also investigated to account for social, sociological, neuro-physiological, and biomechanical perspectives (Wiemeyer et al. 2016: 253).

The report by Wiemeyer et al. (2016), while extensive, could be complemented by further related phenomena, like a construct of game approachability – the degree to which users are intrigued enough to pick particular VG titles for the first time in their life, marking a beginning of their user motivation schema. Perhaps a more concrete example, however, would be that players game for specific values, seeking out titles that are more or less profound or artful, ones that allow them to relax and destress, reduce negative states of mind, or conversely ones that provide them with challenges or an opportunity to compete among other players, or to socialise with friends or strangers. Indeed, one well-known 1996 classification by Richard Bartle of gameplaying motivation, which stems from role-playing multi-user dungeon (*MUDs*) playstyles, identifies 'four primary categories of players (achievers, explorers, socialisers and killers)'; however, this is seen as controversial in terms of empirical refinement (Johnson & Gardner 2010: 1; Kallio et al. 2011: 329). Nonetheless, a comprehensive meta-synthesis of player types offered by Juho Hamari and Janne Tuunanen

(2014: 46), after investigating several previous ways that play motivation has been typified, found grounds for grouping the dimensions into achievement, exploration, sociability, domination, and immersion – further complementing them with the intensity of the mode of play, and suggesting additional behavioural measurements.

Other ways of typifying play motivation exist. Daniel Johnson and John Gardner (2010: 2) formed part of a research programme on possible links between motivation and personality by operationalising motivation through several measures in the Player Experience of Need Satisfaction model, namely 'competence, autonomy, relatedness, intuitive controls and presence/immersion'. Kallio, Mäyrä, and Kaipainen (2011: 335–336), on the other hand, introduced a gaming mentality heuristics framework which aims to be appreciative of gaming as a diversely meaningful activity that is 'rapidly becoming a part of everyone's everyday life everywhere in the world', partitioning it into points like the length and regularity of use sessions, levels of concentration, sociability (cooperative, competitive, taking turns, advising, keeping company) in the same physical, virtual, or conceptual (sharing experiences, knowledge, views, tips) spaces, or motivations to engage with specific characteristics of games, genres, devices, series, and so on – thus mapping at least nine general reasons to play.

The users' willingness to utilise the unique customisability of multimodal interactive software may also be at play here. Choosing to play the same VG title with or without other players might drastically change its reception. Likewise, VGs tend to lock gameplay segments or storylines behind in-game challenges and difficult feats. A popular example of this would be the Dark Souls series (FromSoftware 2011). Another variable is the willingness of users to hack their games or to install mods that further customise their experience. Perhaps a more historically well-nested area of VG modifiability, however, is the difficulty settings on which the players can *choose to* engage the game. A popular belief is that both greatly alter the overall experience of VGs – on a spectrum from enjoying the interactive plot to engaging in ludic challenges. As an illustration, *Deus Ex: Human Revolution* (Eidos-Montréal 2011), an immersive sim [genre specialising in empowering player's decision-making through robust and interwoven simulation systems], offers players a choice of difficulty as either *Tell Me a Story* or *Give Me a Challenge*. But an even earlier cyberpunk immersive sim *System Shock* (Looking Glass Technologies 1994) presented players with options regarding four different difficulty areas, amounting to four different aspects of gameplay (combat, mission, puzzles, mini-games): disabling features, simplifying them, or making them more troublesome – all compared to the default developer-intended setting.

Notably, difficulty setup and other settings that favour player decision-making to customise their experience to their needs often directly translates into cognitive and motor accessibility features as well. A particular case of this is *Celeste* (Extremely OK Games 2018) – a fast-paced platforming game whose themes revolve around conquering one's weaknesses. As the game itself states, '*Celeste* is intended to be a challenging and rewarding experience'. However, it continues this in the following way: 'If the default game proves inaccessible to you, we hope that you can still find that experience with *Assist Mode*'. This game mode is a set of accessibility *and* difficulty toggles which 'modify the game's rules to fit your specific needs' – more precisely, make the action of the game slower and/or more forgiving (Celeste Wiki 2023).

Players might moreover be more or less compelled to engage in in-game behaviour that utilises features that were *not* implemented in the game intentionally: cheats, bugs, glitches, or game-system exploits. Users might use those for humorous, disruptive, or subversive effects. A popular example comes from *The Elder Scrolls V: Skyrim* (Bethesda Game Studios 2011) where it was possible to conceal the eyes of diegetic shopkeepers by placing various receptacles (buckets, clay pots) on their character model's heads, since the game was not programmed to react to such a situation. Because the keeper's scripted line of sight was broken, the player's avatar could be instructed to shoplift without facing the consequences of being caught red-handed (McMullen 2021). Such emersive (Kubiński 2014) in-game actions, regardless (or maybe even *because*) of their non-sensical interpretability on the semiotic level (Bernal-Merino 2016a), point to VGs being a ludic medium unlike films or books – despite all of them providing users with high-fidelity music, realistic graphics, and plenty of meaningful written texts.

5 Conclusions

The three sets of parameters we discussed in Section 2 (*user experience facets*), Section 3 (*translated games facets*), and Section 4 (*game users facets*) can be represented as the blueprint in Figure 16, outlining *game translation user research.*[7] Researchers can use the blueprint to guide study design, starting from for example *facets of user experience* when planning tools and methods for measurement of the dependent variables and effects studied in users, *facets of translated games* when preparing the materials, priming stimuli, and manipulated variables, and *facets of users* to consult potential covariates, control variables, or independent variables. *Facets of translated*

---

[7] We propose *GTUR* as an abbreviation – similar to *GUR* (cf. Drachen et al. 2018), *CTIS* (cf. Olalla-Soler et al. 2021), *UCT* (cf. Suojanen et al. 2015), etc.

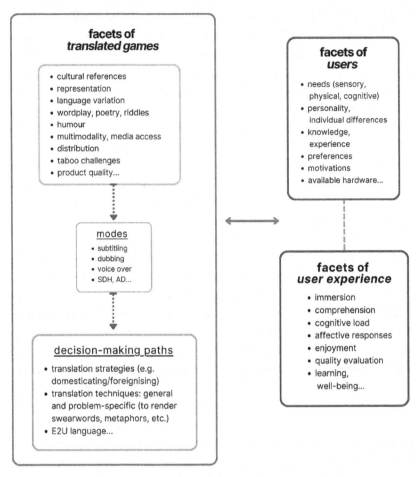

Figure 16 A facets-based mapping of possible parameters in game translation user research.

games are influencing the *facets of users* long-term and *facets of user experience* in a more immediate fashion, and both *facets of user experience* and *facets of users* can be considered in direct relationship to one another. For brevity and clarity, some facets discussed in detail throughout the Element are collapsed into hypernymic labels on the blueprint. More importantly, some facets visible in Figure 16 have not been discussed in detail in the Element (e.g. quality of the product/translation as a *facet of translated games*). The blueprint aims to illustrate that even more parameters are available under the proposed three-pronged relationship and the blueprint can be extended if brand new parameters become relevant for game translation user research, to be mapped in any of the three sets of facets.

Regina Bernhaupt opened her handbook on Human–Computer Interaction enumerating some major goals for game development: to create aesthetically moving experiences that are entertaining, full of surprises, but which also allow players to learn and overcome, and which 'support social connectedness or allow the player to identify with the game' (Bernhaupt 2015: 1). The game translation user research (GTUR) that we outline in this Element operates on the same set of premises, but complements them with protocols from reception studies (cf. e.g. Di Giovanni & Gambier 2018). Thus, it runs parallel to what Chmiel and Mazur (2012: 58) expressed in the context of media accessibility reception studies: the inclusion of AVT end-users by focusing on their feedback can not only 'directly contribute to the quality' of the product, but also generate new perspectives on the 'strategies and solutions' of the process. Should the emerging field of localisation-user research be considered an interconnected part of a larger, well-recognised framework already in place, like GUR? If we assume that 'any aspect of a video game that influences the user's experience and perception of that game is of concern' for GUR (Drachen et al. 2018: 1), then GILT practices, with their explicit aim of trying to preserve the source-text experience[8] (O'Hagan & Mangiron 2004: 57), seems like an obvious constituent. Because GUR operates across all phases of VG creation, 'from early designs, through prototypes, and after launch', the adoption of localisation-user research within the frameworks of GUR can be seen as directly related to the postulates of Pablo Romero-Fresco's (2019: 6) about filmmaking. Linguistic experts can be incorporated into media development workflows, 'to reveal to them the often unknown aspects of how their [games] are changed [by introducing them to new locales through translation]'.

While we recognise that the paradigms are already shifting, it is possible to extend Romero-Fresco's ideas to the broader media landscape – and games development, subsequently. He explicitly states that the motivation is 'not to compromise the [media] makers' vision or constrain their freedom', but to instead 'help to preserve [the intended media experiences] across different audiences' through a more users-oriented collaboration (Romero-Fresco 2019: 6). In other words, game authors, armed with the awareness of how games are experienced on a global scale and by different users, can be aided by linguistic experts. The maturing game industry started last decade to put into practice internationalisation, glocalisation, and accessibility theories embracing co-creation and shared-authorship across their

---

[8] 'The main priority of game localization is to ensure that the gamer experience of the localized product is similar to that of the source language product player' – typically necessitating the deployment of processes beyond just language-transfer of textual messages, for example proper rendering of challenge, assets, animations, humour, and many other (O'Hagan & Mangiron 2004: 60).

teams (Mangiron & O'Hagan 2006) with considerable improvements in playability and immersion for all kinds of players around the world (Bernal-Merino 2016b, 2020).

Research into VG reception is still fragmented. On the one hand, scholars can benefit from the area of Game User Research which seems to have evolved from wedding industry-intensive fields like *Game Design, Development (GameDev), Game Analytics (GA), User Experience Evaluation/Assessment,* and *Game Localisation (L10 N,* cf. *language service provision, LSP*), with the more academically driven ones like *Games Research, Computer Science,* or *Affective Ludology.* On the other, there is still a wealth of research in *Psychometrics, Media Reception, Human–Computer Interaction (HCI), Audiovisual Translation* and *Media Accessibility,* and more. It seems that a more unified area is emerging.

References

5th Cell (2009). *Scribblenauts* [American and British English language versions]. Warner Bros. Interactive Entertainment.

Abeele, V. V., Spiel, K., Nacke, L., Johnson, D., & Gerling, K. (2020). Development and validation of the player experience inventory: A scale to measure player experiences at the level of functional and psychosocial consequences. *International Journal of Human-Computer Studies*, 135, 1–12. https://DOI.org/ggjqff

AD4Games (2021). *August 2021 – Live Audio Description of the Game 'Before I Forget'*. YouTube. https://youtu.be/1oY_-Zx9z90

Adlan, W. A. (2020). *Larian Studios Talks about 'The Larian Way'*. Gamer Braves. www.gamerbraves.com/level-up-kl-2020-larian-studios-talks-about-the-larian-way/

Afzali, K. & Zahiri, M. (2022). A netnographic exploration of Iranian video-game players translation needs: The case of in-game texts. *The Translator*, 28(1), 74–94, https://doi.org/10.1080/13556509.2021.1880536

Al-Batineh, M. & Alawneh, R. (2022). Current trends in localizing video games into Arabic: Localization levels and gamers' preferences. *Perspectives: Studies in Translation Theory and Practice*, 30(2), pp. 323–342. https://doi.org/10.1080/0907676X.2021.1926520

Almeida, S., Veloso, A., Roque, L., & Mealha, O. (2011). The Eyes and Games: A Survey of Visual Attention and Eye Tracking Input in Video Games. *Proceedings of SBGames*, 1–10. https://sbgames.org/sbgames2011/proceedings/sbgames/papers/

Arasu, P. (2023). *Hogwarts Legacy's Game Mechanics Reflect the Gender Essentialism at the Heart of Harry Potter*. The Conversation. https://theconversation.com/hogwarts-legacys-game-mechanics-reflect-the-gender-essentialism-at-the-heart-of-harry-potter-199604

Atlus (1996). *Revelations: Persona* (North American release). Atlus USA.

Babbie, E. R. (2021). *Practice of Social Research*. Boston: Cengage Learning.

Bardini, F. (2020). Film language, film emotions and the experience of blind and partially sighted viewers: A reception study. *The Journal of Specialised Translation* 33, 259–280.

Barnes, W. (2012). *Starcraft 2: Carte Blanche Localization*. Localization Summit, Game Developers Conference. San Francisco. www.gdcvault.com/play/1015645/StarCraft-II-Carte-Blanche

Bartelt-Krantz, M. (2017). Game localization management: Balancing linguistic quality and financial efficiency. *TRANS. Revista De Traductología* 15: 83–88. ISSN 1137-2311. https://doi.org/10.24310/TRANS.2011.v0i15.3197.

Bartle, R. (1996). *Hearts, Clubs, Diamonds, Spades: Players Who Suit MUDs*. Richard Bartle. www.mud.co.uk/richard/hcds.htm.

Bernabé-Caro, R., Orero, P., García, Ó., & Oncins, E. (2020). Validation of easy-to-read subtitles. In D. Dejica, C. Eugeni, & A. Dejica-Cartis (Eds.), *Translation Studies and Information Technology – New Pathways for Researchers, Teachers and Professionals* (pp. 162–175). Timişoara: Timişoara Editura Politehnica.

Bernal-Merino, M. Á. (2015). *Translation and Localisation in Video Games: Making Entertainment Software Global*. New York: Routledge.

Bernal-Merino, M. Á. (2016a). Creating felicitous gaming experiences: Semiotics and pragmatics as tools for video game localisation. *Signata*, 7, 231–253. https://doi.org/10/gmzm38

Bernal-Merino, M. Á. (2016b). The glocalization and co-creation in video games. In D. Thussu (Ed.), *Media across Borders: Localizing TV, Film and Video Games* (pp. 202–219). New York: Routledge.

Bernal-Merino, M. Á. (2018a). Creativity and playability in the localisation of video games. *The Journal of Internationalization and Localization*, 5(1), 75–96.

Bernal-Merino, M. Á. (2018b). Quantum identity and the enhancement of communication. *Journal of Brand Strategy*, 6(4), 380–391. London: Henry Stewart.

Bernal-Merino, M. Á. (2020). Key concepts in game localisation quality. In Ł. Bogucki & M. Deckert (Eds.), *The Palgrave Handbook of Audiovisual Translation and Media Accessibility* (pp. 297–314). Cham: Springer International. https://doi.org/10.1007/978-3-030-42105-2_15

Bernhaupt, R. (2015). User experience evaluation methods in the games development life cycle. In R. Bernhaupt (Ed.), *Game User Experience Evaluation (Human–Computer Interaction Series)* (pp. 1–8). New York: Springer. https://doi.org/10.1007/978-3-319-15985-0_1

Bethesda Game Studios (2008). *Fallout 3*. Bethesda Softworks.

Bethesda Game Studios (2011). *The Elder Scrolls V: Skyrim*. Bethesda Softworks.

Bethesda Game Studios (2023). *Starfield*. Bethesda Softworks.

Blizzard Entertainment (2010). *StarCraft II: Wings of Liberty* (English original, Russian and Korean localisation). Blizzard Entertainment.

Blizzard Entertainment (2014). *Hearthstone* (English original, Spanish localisation). Blizzard. https://news.blizzard.com/es-es/hearthstone/15019545/la-traduccion-de-hearthstone-un-vistazo-desde-dentro

Blizzard Entertainment (2016). *Overwatch* (various language versions). Blizzard Entertainment.

Bogost, I. (2011). *How to Do Things with Videogames*. Minnesota: University of Minnesota Press.

Bogost, I. (2015). *How to Talk about Videogames*. Minnesota: University of Minnesota Press.

Brigstow Institute. (2021). *AD4Games: making video games accessible for visually impaired players – Brigstow Institute*. University of Bristol. https://brigstowinstitute.blogs.bristol.ac.uk/project/ad4games/.

Brown, E. & Cairns, P. (2004). A grounded investigation of game immersion. *Extended Abstracts of the 2004 Conference on Human Factors and Computing Systems – CHI '04*, 1297–1300. https://doi.org/10.1145/985921.986048

Cavia (2010a). *Nier Replicant*. Square Enix.

Cavia (2010b). *Nier Gestalt*. Square Enix.

CD Projekt Red (2015). *The Witcher 3: Wild Hunt*. CD Projekt.

Celeste Wiki (2023). Assist Mode [Community-curated]. https://celeste.ink/wiki/Assist_Mode

Chau, J. (2019, 13 September). *The Success of Multi-Billion Dollar Free-to-Play Games Isn't Culture*. Medium. https://medium.com/@SJeneris/the-success-of-multi-billion-dollar-free-to-play-games-isnt-culture-474195d212a2

Chebat, D. R., Schneider, F. C., Kupers, R., & Ptito, M. (2011). Navigation with a sensory substitution device in congenitally blind individuals. *Neuroreport*, 7(22), 342–347. https://doi.org/10.1097/wnr.0b013e3283462def

Chmiel, A. & Mazur, I. (2012). AD reception research: Some methodological considerations. In E. Perego (Ed.), *Emerging Topics in Translation: Audio Description* (pp. 57–80). Trieste: EUT Edizioni Università di Trieste. http://hdl.handle.net/10077/6361

Chu, M. (2017). *Thinking Globally: Building the Optimistic Future of 'Overwatch'*. GDC Vault. www.gdcvault.com/play/1024266/Thinking-Globally-Building-the-Optimistic

Crosignani, S. (2011). *Tips for Successful Games Audio Production*. MultiLingual, https://multilingual.com/articles/tips-for-successful-games-audio-production

Crosignani, S. & Ravetto, F. (2011). Localizing the buzz! Game series (Or how to successfully implement transcreation in a multi-million seller video game). *TRANS: Revista de Traductología15*. Special issue on games localization, 29–38.

Csikszentmihalyi, M. (1990). *Flow: The Psychology of Optimal Experience*. New York: Harper & Row.

d'Ydewalle, G., Muylle, P., & van Rensbergen, J. (1985). Attention shifts in partially redundant information situations. In R. Groner, G. W. McConkie, & C. Menz (Eds.), *Eye Movements and Human Information Processing* (pp. 375–384). North-Holland: Elsevier.

d'Ydewalle, G., Van Rensbergen, J., & Pollet, J. (1987). Reading a message when the same message is available auditorily in another language: The case of subtitling. In J. K. O'Reagan & A. Lévy Schoen (Eds.), *Eye Movements: From Physiology to Cognition* (pp. 313–321), Amsterdam: Elsevier Science Publishers B.V.

Dale, L. (2023, 11 August). *The Switch 2 NEEDS These Accessibility Improvements.* Access-Ability. https://access-ability.uk/2023/08/11/the-switch-2-needs-these-accessibility-improvements/

Deck Nine (2021). *Life Is Strange: True Colors.* Square Enix. https://lifeis strange.square-enix-games.com/en-us/

Deckert, M. (2021). Język w przestrzeni ekranu: Przekładowe nieoczywiste oczywistości. In P. Stalmaszczyk (Ed.), *Język(i) w czasie i przestrzeni* (pp. 99–115). Łódź: University of Lodz Press. https://wydawnictwo.uni.lodz.pl/produkt/jezyki-w-czasie-i-przestrzeni

Deckert, M. & Hejduk, K. W. (2022a). *On-Screen Language in Video Games: A Translation Perspective.* Cambridge: Cambridge University Press.

Deckert, M. & Hejduk, K. W. (2022b). Videogame localisation, spelling errors and player reception. *Translation, Cognition & Behavior*, 5(1), 27–49. https://doi.org/h422

Deckert, M. & Hejduk, K. W. (2024). Can video game subtitling shape player satisfaction? *Perspectives: Studies in Translation Theory and Practice* 32(1), 59–75. https://doi.org/jp9m

Di Giovanni, E. (2020). Reception studies and audiovisual translation. In Ł. Bogucki & M. Deckert (Eds.), *The Palgrave Handbook of Audiovisual Translation and Media Accessibility* (pp. 397–413). Amsterdam: Springer International. https://doi.org/10.1007/978-3-030-42105-2_20

Di Giovanni, E. & Gambier, Y. (Eds.). (2018). *Reception Studies and Audiovisual Translation.* Amsterdam: John Benjamins.

Dontnod Entertainment, Deck Nine, Square Enix (2015–2022). *Life Is Strange [series].* Square Enix.

Downs, J., Vetere, F., Howard, S., & Loughnan, S. (2013). Measuring audience experience in social videogaming. *Proceedings of the 25th Australian Computer-Human Interaction Conference: Augmentaiton, Application, Innovation, Collaboration, 25.* https://doi.org/10.1145/2541016.2541054

Drachen, A., Mirza-Babaei, P., & Nacke, L. E. (Eds.). (2018). *Game User Research.* Oxford: Oxford University Press.

Eidos-Montréal (2011). *Deus Ex: Human Revolution*. Square Enix.

Eidos-Montréal (2018). *Shadow of the Tomb Raider*. Square Enix.

Electronic Arts (2022, 4 August). *Customizable Pronouns Now Available in the Sims 4*. EA. www.ea.com/en/games/the-sims/the-sims-4/news/customizable-pronouns-now-available-in-the-sims-4

Ellefsen, U. (2015). *Between Reality and (Science) Fiction: French Localisation of the Post-Apocalyptic American dream*. Unpublished essay, London.

Ellefsen, U. & Bernal-Merino, M. Á. (2018). Harnessing the roar of the crowd: A quantitative study of language preferences in video games of French players of the Northern Hemisphere. *The Journal of Internationalization and Localization* 5(1), 21–48. https://doi.org/kv23

Epic Games (2017). *Fortnite: Battle Royale*. Epic Games.

Epic Games Dev Community (2023). *Fortnite Creative Glossary*. Epic Developer Community. https://dev.epicgames.com/documentation/en-us/fortnite-creative/fortnite-creative-glossary

ESRB (2023). *Life Is Strange: True Colors – ESRB*. ESRB Ratings. www.esrb.org/ratings/37564/life-is-strange-true-colors/

Extremely OK Games (2018). *Celeste*. Extremely OK Games.

Faure, Q. (2020). *Pokémon, traduisez-les tous?: L'impact de la localisation sur l'expérience des joueurs: comparaison des versions française et italiennes des jeux vidéo Pokémon* (Master's dissertation). Geneva: University of Geneva.

Fernández-Costales, A. (2016). Analyzing players' perceptions on the translation of video games: Assessing the tension between the local and the global concerning language use. In A. Esser, M. Á. Bernal-Merino, and I. R. Smith (Eds.), *Media Across Borders: Localizing TV, Film, and Video Games* (pp. 183–201). New York: Routledge.

Ferrara, J. (2012). *Playful Design: Creating Game Experiences in Everyday Interfaces*. New York: Rosenfeld Media.

FIFA (2023). *The Football Landscape – The Vision 2020–2023*. FIFA. https://publications.fifa.com/en/vision-report-2021/the-football-landscape/

Forums Blizzard (2022, 14 October). *Frases mal traducidas*. Overwatch Forums (Spanish); Blizzard. https://eu.forums.blizzard.com/es/overwatch/t/frases-mal-traducidas/12082

Freeman, M. & Rampazzo, G. R. (2018). *The Routledge Companion to Transmedia Studies*. New York: Routledge.

Frijda, N. H. (2007a). Klaus Scherer's article on 'what are emotions?' Comments. *Social Science Information*, 46(3), 381–383. https://doi.org/10.1177/0539018407079694

Frijda, N. H. (2007b). What might emotions be? Comments on the Comments. *Social Science Information*, 46(3), 433–443. https://doi.org/10.1177/0539018 4070460030112

FromSoftware (2011). *Dark Souls* [series]. Bandai Namco Entertainment.

Galdra Studios (2021). *Arcadia Fallen*. Galdra Studios.

Game Accessibility Guidelines (2023). *Game Accessibility Guidelines | Full List*. Game Accessibility Guidelines. https://gameaccessibilityguidelines .com/full-list/

Game User Interaction and Intelligence Lab (2022, 25 September). *Official Website of GUII Lab's Game User Research Methods Project; Game User Interaction and Intelligence Lab*. Santa Cruz: University of California. https://gur.ucsc.edu

GameTec (2022). *Overwatch 2 ALL Characters Ultimate Voice Lines (with Subtitles) HD*. YouTube. www.youtube.com/watch?v=jt6jFU4Rs_M

Garda, M. B. (2012). Limits of genre, limits of fantasy: Rethinking computer role-playing games. In A. L. Brackin & N. Guyot (Eds.), *Cultural Perspectives of Video Games: From Designer to Player* (pp. 91–99). Leiden: Brill. https://doi.org/10.1163/9781848881617_010

Gerblick, J. (2021, 20 October). *Over 20,000 Sims 4 Players Ask EA to Add Gender-Neutral Pronouns*. Games Radar. www.gamesradar.com/over-20000-sims-4-players-ask-ea-to-add-gender-neutral-pronouns/

Geurts, F. (2015). What do you want to play? *The Desirability of Video Game Translations from English into Dutch according to Dutch Gamers and Non-gamers* (Master's Dissertation). Leiden: Leiden University. https://studentth eses.universiteitleiden.nl/handle/1887/34704

Greco, G. M. (2016). On accessibility as a human right, with an application to media accessibility. In A. Matamala & P. Orero (Eds.), *Researching Audio Description: New approaches* (pp. 11–33). London: Palgrave Macmillan.

Guerrilla Games & Firesprite (2017–2023). *Horizon [series]*. Sony Interactive Entertainment.

Haider, A., Harteveld, C., Johnson, D., et al. (2022). miniPXI: Development and validation of an eleven-item measure of the player experience inventory. *Proceedings of the ACM on Human-Computer Interaction, 6(CHI PLAY)*, 1–26. https://doi.org/10.1145/3549507

Hamari, J. & Tuunanen, J. (2014). Player types: A meta-synthesis. *Transactions of the Digital Games Research Association*, 1(2), 29–53. https://doi.org/10/ ggp9fk

Harkin, M. (2023). *Brazilian Gamers Get Local | MultiLingual July 2023*. Multilingual.com. https://multilingual.com/issues/july-2023/brazilian-gamers-get-local/

Hart, A. (2022, 15 December). *Baldur's Gate 3 Adds Non-binary Option.* Gayming Magazine. https://gaymingmag.com/2022/12/baldurs-gate-3-adds-non-binary-option/

Harteveld, C., Javvaji, N., Machado, T., et al. (2020). Preliminary development and evaluation of the mini player experience inventory (mPXI). *CHI PLAY '20: Extended Abstracts of the 2020 Annual Symposium on Computer-Human Interaction in Play.* https://doi.org/10.1145/3383668.3419877

Hejduk, K. W. (2022). *A Multimethod Approach to On-Screen Language Localisation Reception – the Case of a Logical Adventure Video Game* (Unpublished master's dissertation). Łódź: University of Lodz.

Hernandez, M. (2017). *Video Game Localisation: A Francophone Gamers' Perspective on the Quality of PC Video Game Localisation* (Master's dissertation). University of Geneva.

Hsieh, H. F. & Shannon, S. E. (2005). Three approaches to qualitative content analysis. *Qualitative Health Research*, 15(9), 1277–1288. https://doi.org/10.1177/1049732305276687

Huizinga, J. (1955). *Homo Ludens: A Study of the Play-Element in Culture.* Boston: Beacon Press.

IGDA Game Accessibility Special Interest Group (2021, 26 August). *The IGDA Game Accessibility Special Interest Group Homepage.* IGDA Game Accessibility SIG; IGDA. https://igda-gasig.org/

IGDA Games Research and User Experience SIG (2023, 16 August). *Official Website of IGDA Games Research & User Experience.* International Game Developers Association Games Research and User Experience Special Interest Group. https://grux.org/grux-sig

Impey, S. (2018). *Mobile vs Desktop UI: Key Differences In Design.* GameAnalytics. https://gameanalytics.com/blog/mobile-desktop-ui-design/

International Game Developers Association (2020). *Official Website of the International Game Developers Association.* IGDA. https://igda.org/

Internet Society Foundation (2023, 15 May). *What Are the Most Used Languages on the Internet?* www.isocfoundation.org/2023/05/what-are-the-most-used-languages-on-the-internet/

Interplay (1997). *Fallout: A Post Nuclear Role Playing Game.* Interplay.

Ishii, R. (2022, 30 March). *Ghostwire: Tokyo Is Filled with Humor Most Players Won't Understand.* Automaton Media. https://automaton-media.com/en/reviews/20220330-10937/

Isometricorp Games (2022). *Tunic.* Finji.

Izard, C. E. (2009). Emotion theory and research: Highlights, unanswered questions, and emerging issues. *Annual Review of Psychology*, 60(1), 1–25. https://doi.org/10.1146/annurev.psych.60.110707.163539

Japan Studio & Team Ico (2001). *Ico*. Sony Computer Entertainment.

Jiménez-Crespo, M. A. (2018). Localisation research in translation studies. In H. Dam, M. Brøgger, & K. Zethsen (Eds.), *Moving Boundaries in Translation Studies* (pp. 26–44). London: Routledge. https://doi.org/10.4324/978131 5121871-3

Johnson, D. & Gardner, J. (2010). Personality, motivation and video games. *Proceedings of the 22nd Conference of the Computer-Human Interaction Special Interest Group of Australia on Computer-Human Interaction – OZCHI '10.* https://doi.org/10.1145/1952222.1952281

Johnson, D., Wyeth, P., Sweetser, P., & Gardner, J. (2012). Personality, genre and videogame play experience. *Proceedings of the 4th International Conference on Fun and Games – FnG '12.* https://doi.org/10.1145/2367616 .2367633

Kabát, M. (2023). Factors influencing the quality of digital game localization. *Acta Ludologica*, 6(1), 84–94. https://doi.org/10.34135/actaludologica.2023-6-1.84-94

Kallio, K. P., Mäyrä, F., & Kaipainen, K. (2011). At least nine ways to play: Approaching gamer mentalities. *Games and Culture*, 6(4), 327–353. https://doi.org/10/fv6hqp

Keebler, J. R., Shelstad, W. J., Smith, D. C., Chaparro, B. S., & Phan, M. H. (2020). Validation of the GUESS-18: A short version of the game user experience satisfaction scale (GUESS)JUX. *Journal of User Experience*, 16(1), 49–62. https://uxpajournal.org/validation-game-user-experience-satis faction-scale-guess/

Khaliq, I. & Dela Torre, I. (2019). A study on accessibility in games for the visually impaired. In A. Bujari, P. Manzoni, A. Forster, E. Mota, & O. Gaggi (Eds.), *Proceedings of the 5th EAI International Conference on Smart Objects and Technologies for Social Good*, pp. 142–148. New York: Association for Computing Machinery ACM Digital Library. https://doi .org/10.1145/3342428.3342682

Khoshsaligheh, M. & Ameri, S. (2020). Video game localisation in Iran: A survey of users' profile, gaming habits and preferences. *The Translator*, 26(2), 190–208.

Koscelníková, M. (2021). The localization of video games into less widely spoken languages that share a common history. *The Journal of Internationalization and Localization*, 8(1), 1–25. https://doi.org/10.1075/ jial.20013.kos

Kotaku (2018). *Assassin's Creed: Origins' Tour Mode Censors Naked Statues*. Kotaku. www.kotaku.com.au/2018/02/assassins-creed-origins-tour-mode-censors-naked-statues

Kozinets, R. (2010). *Netnography: Doing Ethnographic Research Online.* California: Sage.

Kruger, J.-L. (2019). Eye tracking in audiovisual translation research, in L. Pérez-González (Ed.), *The Routledge Handbook of Audiovisual Translation* (pp. 350–366). New York: Routledge.

Kruger, J.-L., Hefer, E., & Matthew, G. (2013). Measuring the impact of subtitles on cognitive load. *Proceedings of the 2013 Conference on Eye Tracking South Africa – ETSA '13.* https://doi.org/10.1145/2509315.2509331

Kruger, J.-L., Hefer, E., & Matthew, G. (2014). Attention distribution and cognitive load in a subtitled academic lecture: L1 vs. L2. *Journal of Eye Movement Research,* 7(5), 1–15. https://doi.org/10.16910/jemr.7.5.4

Kruger, J.-L., Szarkowska, A., & Krejtz, I. (2015). Subtitles on the moving image: An overview of eye tracking studies. *Refractory: A Journal of Entertainment Media,* 25, 1–14.

Kubiński, P. (2014). Immersion vs. emersive effects in videogames. In D. Stobbart & M. Evans (Eds.), *Engaging with Videogames: Play, Theory and Practice* (pp. 133–141). Leiden: Brill. https://doi.org/10.1163/97818 48882959_013

Kudła, D. (2020). *Ocena odbioru lokalizacji językowej gier komputerowych na podstawie danych okulograficznych.* Warsaw: Institute of Specialised and Intercultural Communication.

Kudła, D. (2021). The views of dedicated Polish gamers on the localization of video games into Polish – online survey results. *Kwartalnik Neofilologiczny* LXVIII, 4, 530–549. https://doi.org/10.24425/kn.2021.139558

Lagunes-Ramirez, D., González-Serna, G., Lopez-Sanchez, M., et al. (2020). Study of the user's eye tracking to analyze the blinking behavior while playing a video game to identify cognitive load levels. *2020 IEEE International Autumn Meeting on Power, Electronics and Computing (ROPEC).* https://doi.org/10.1109/ropec50909.2020.9258693

Larian Studios (2023). *Baldur's Gate 3.* Larian Studios.

Larreina-Morales, M. E., & Mangiron, C. (2023). Audio description in video games? Persons with visual disabilities weigh in. *Universal Access in the Information Society.* https://doi.org/10.1007/s10209-023-01036-4

Lee, J. (2008). *Fallout 3 withheld from India: Microsoft India Cancels the Title's Release over Fears of Offending 'Cultural Sensitivities'.* Game Industry Biz. www.gamesindustry.biz/fallout-3-withheld-from-india

Lemhöfer, K. & Broersma, M. (2011). Introducing LexTALE: A quick and valid lexical test for advanced learners of English. *Behavior Research Methods,* 44(2), 325–343. https://doi.org/10.3758/s13428-011-0146-0

Live Wire (2022). *Harvestella.* Square Enix.

Logitech (2023). *Logitech G Adaptive Gaming Kit for the Xbox Adaptive Controller*. LogitechG Commercial Website. www.logitechg.com/en-us/prod ucts/gamepads/adaptive-gaming-kit-accessories.943-000318.html

Looking Glass Technologies (1994). *System Shock*. Origin Systems.

Makkonen, J. (2015/2017). *Distraint: Deluxe Edition*. Jesse Makkonen [independent creator].

Mandiberg, S. (2018). Fallacies of game localization: Censorship and #TorrentialDownpour. *The Journal of Internationalization and Localization*, 4, 162–182.

Mangiron, C. (2010). The importance of not being earnest: Translating humour in video games. In D. Chiaro (Ed.), *Translation, Humour and the Media: Translation and Humour*, volume 2 (pp. 89–107). London: Bloomsbury. https://www.bloomsbury.com/us/translation-humour-and-the-media-9781441137883/.

Mangiron, C. (2013). Subtitling in game localisation: A descriptive study. *Perspectives: Studies in Translatology* 21(1), 42–56. https://doi.org/10.1080/0907676X.2012.722653

Mangiron, C. (2016). Reception of game subtitles: An empirical study. *The Translator* 22(1), 72–93. https://doi.org/10.1080/13556509.2015.1110000

Mangiron, C. (2017). Research in game localization: An overview. *The Journal of Internationalization and Localization*, 4(2), 74–99.

Mangiron, C. (2018a). Game on! Burning issues in game localisation. *Journal of Audiovisual Translation*, 1(1), 122–138. https://doi.org/10.47476/jat.v1i1.48

Mangiron, C. (2018b). Reception studies in game localisation: Taking stock. In E. Di Giovanni & Y. Gambier (Eds.), *Reception Studies and Audiovisual Translation* (pp. 277–296). Amsterdam: John Benjamins. https://doi.org/10.1075/btl.141.14man

Mangiron, C. (2021). Game accessibility: Taking inclusion to the next level. In M. Antona & C. Stephanidis (Eds.), *Universal Access in Human-Computer Interaction. Design Methods and User Experience. HCII 2021. Lecture Notes in Computer Science*, volume 12768 (pp. 269–279). Cham: Springer. https://doi.org/10.1007/978-3-030-78092-0_17

Mangiron, C. & O'Hagan, M. (2006). Game localisation: Unleashing imagination with 'restricted' translation. *The Journal of Specialised Translation*, 6, 10–21.

Mangiron, C. & Zhang, X. (2016). Game accessibility for the blind: Current overview and the potential application of audio description as the way forward. In A. Matamala & P. Orero (Eds.), *Researching Audio Description* (pp. 75–95). London: Palgrave Macmillan.

Mangiron, C. & Zhang, X. (2022). Video games and audio description. In C. Taylor & E. Perego (Eds.), *The Routledge Handbook of Audio Description* (pp. 377–390). New York: Routledge. https://doi.org/10.4324/9781003003052-29

Matamala, A. (2021). Accessibility in 360° videos: Methodological aspects and main results of evaluation activities in the ImAc project. *Sendebar*, 32, 65–89.

Matamala, A. (2022). Easy-to-understand language in audiovisual translation and accessibility: State of the art and future challenges. *XLinguae*, 15(2), 130–144. https://doi.org/10.18355/XL.2022.15.02.10

Matamala, A., Soler-Vilageliu, O., Iturregui-Gallardo, G., et al. (2020). Electrodermal activity as a measure of emotions in media accessibility research: Methodological considerations. *The Journal of Specialised Translation*, 33, 129–151.

Maxwell-Chandler, H. & O'Malley-Deming, S. (2012). *The Game Localization Handbook* (2nd ed.). Sudbury: Jones & Bartlett Learning.

McEvoy, J. (2021, 10 December). *Fortnite Slang and Terms Explained*. Know Your Mobile. www.knowyourmobile.com/user-guides/fortnite-slang-and-terms-explained/

McLaughlin, M. & Muñoz-Basols, J. (Eds.). (2021). *Ideology, Censorship and Translation*. New York: Routledge. https://doi.org/10.4324/9781003102793

McMullen, C. (2021). *Skyrim's Bucket Robbery Is a Testament to Player Creativity*. The Escapist. www.escapistmagazine.com/skyrim-bucket-robbery-is-a-testament-to-player-creativity/

Mejías-Climent, L. (2017). The multiple (translatable) factors of a video game. In A. Bécart, V. Merola, & R. López-Campo Bodineau (Eds.), *New Technologies Applied to Translation Studies: Strategies, Tools and Resources* (pp. 83–90). Seville: Editorial Bienza.

Mejías-Climent, L. (2021). Recepción de los productos accesibles y la formación de subtituladores: Personas sordas en el aula de SPS. *Quaderns: Revista de Traducció*, 28, 255–270. https://doi.org/10.5565/rev/quaderns.43

Mejías-Climent, L. (2022). *Enhancing Video Game Localization through Dubbing*. Cham: Palgrave Macmillan. https://doi.org/10.1007/978-3-030-88292-1

Mescon, S. (2011). *League of Legends: What It Means to Be Player-Focused*. GDC Vault. www.gdcvault.com/play/1015040/League-of-Legends-What-it

MidBoss (2015). *2064: Read Only Memories*. Limited Run Games.

Morin, S. M. (2021, 25 May). *8 Differences between Nier Gestalt and Nier Replicant*. TheGamer. www.thegamer.com/nier-replicant-gestalt-games-comparison/

Mortal Kombat Wiki (2023). *Mortal Kombat 11* [Community-curated]. FANDOM Games Community. https://mortalkombat.fandom.com/wiki/Mortal_Kombat_11

Nacke, L. E. & Lindley, C. A. (2009). Affective Ludology, Flow and Immersion in a First-Person Shooter: Measurement of Player Experience. *Loading ... The Journal of the Canadian Game Studies Association*, 3(5), 1–21. https://journals.sfu.ca/loading/index.php/loading/article/view/72

Naughty Dog (2020). *The Last of Us: Part II*. Sony Interactive Entertainment.

Nawrocka, E. B. (2019). Game localization pitfalls: Translating variables and gender. *Beyond Philology an International Journal of Linguistics, Literary Studies and English Language Teaching*, 16(4), 129–155. https://doi.org/10.26881/bp.2019.4.05

Neidhardt, A. & Rüppel, A. (2012). Multiplayer audio-only game: Pong on a massive multichannel loudspeaker system. *7th Audio Mostly Conference: A Conference on Interaction with Sound*, 130–134.

Nettelbeck, H. W. (2020). Comparing audience perceptions of characters in subtitled film. *Journal of Audiovisual Translation*, 3(1), 50–71. https://doi.org/10.47476/jat.v3i1.2020.102

Nimdzi (2018). *Video Game Localization Report*. www.nimdzi.com/video-game-localization/

Nintendo (2001). *Luigi's Mansion*. Nintendo.

O'Hagan, M. (2005). Multidimensional translation: A game plan for audiovisual translation in the age of GILT. *MuTra 2005 – Challenges of Multidimensional Translation: Conference Proceedings*, 76–87.

O'Hagan, M. (2009). Towards a cross-cultural game design: An explorative study in understanding the player experience of a localised Japanese video game. *Journal of Specialised Translation*, 11, 211–233.

O'Hagan, M. (2016). Game localisation as emotion engineering: Methodological exploration. In M. O'Hagan & Q. Zhang (Eds.), *Conflict and Communication: A Changing Asia in a Globalising World* (pp. 81–102). New York: Nova Science.

O'Hagan, M. & Flanagan, M. (2018). Gamer emotions in laughter. *Translation, Cognition & Behavior*, 1(2), 299–318. https://doi.org/10.1075/tcb.00013.oha

O'Hagan, M. & Mangiron, C. (2004). Games localization: When 'arigato' gets lost in translation. *New Zealand Game Developers Conference Proceedings*, 57–62.

O'Hagan, M. & Mangiron, C. (2013). *Game Localization: Translating for the Global Digital Entertainment Industry*. Amsterdam: John Benjamins.

O'Sullivan, E. (1999). Translating Picture. *Signal*, 90, 167–175.

Obsidian Entertainment (2014). *South Park: The Stick of Truth*. Ubisoft. https:// pegi.info/search-pegi?q=South+Park+%3A+The+Stick+of+Truth&op= Search&age%5B%5D=&descriptor%5B%5D=&publisher=&platform%5B% 5D=&release_year%5B%5D=&page=1&form_build_id=form- t3VGJO_dhy713THXwjRW68z-i0mvunxv9Yw24W5QJno&form_id=pegi_ search_form

Olalla-Soler, C., Franco Aixelá, J., & Rovira-Esteva, S. (2021). Mapping cognitive translation and interpreting studies: A bibliometric approach. *Linguistica Antverpiensia, New Series – Themes in Translation Studies*, 19. https://doi.org/10.52034/lanstts.v19i0.542

Oncins, E., Bernabé, R., Montagut, M., & Arnáiz-Uzquiza, V. (2020). Accessible scenic arts and virtual reality: A pilot study in user preferences when reading subtitles in immersive environments. *MonTi*, 12, 214–241. https://doi.org/10.6035/MonTI.2020.12.07

Orrego-Carmona, D. (2019). Audiovisual translation and audience reception. In L. Pérez-González (Ed.), *The Routledge Handbook of Audiovisual Translation* (pp. 367–382). New York: Routledge.

Patridge, S. (2017). Video games and imaginative identification. *The Journal of Aesthetics and Art Criticism*, 75(2), 181–184. https://doi.org/10.1111/jaac .12355

Pearce, C. (2005). Theory wars: An argument against arguments in the so-called Ludology/Narratology debate. *Proceedings of DiGRA 2005 Conference: Changing Views – Worlds in Play*. www.digra.org/digital-library/publica tions/theory-wars-an-argument-against-arguments-in-the-so-called-ludolo gynarratology-debate

Peever, N., Johnson, D., & Gardner, J. (2012). Personality & video game genre preferences. *Proceedings of the 8th Australasian Conference on Interactive Entertainment Playing the System – IE '12*. https://doi.org/10.1145/2336727 .2336747

Perego, E. (Ed.). (2012). *Eye Tracking in Audiovisual Translation*. Rome: Aracne.

Perego, E. (2020). *Accessible Communication: A Cross-Country Journey*. Berlin: Frank & Timme.

Perego, E., Del Missier, F., & Bottiroli, S. (2015). Dubbing versus subtitling in young and older adults: Cognitive and evaluative aspects. *Perspectives: Studies in Translation Theory and Practice*, 23(1), 1–21. https://doi.org/ 10.1080/0907676x.2014.912343

Phakiti, A. (2015). Quantitative research and analysis. In B. Paltridge & A. Phakiti (Eds.), *Research Methods in Applied Linguistics: A Practical Resource* (pp. 34–48). London: Bloomsbury Academic.

Phan, M. H., Keebler J. R., & Chaparro B. S. (2016). The development and validation of the game user experience satisfaction scale (GUESS). *Human Factors: The Journal of the Human Factors and Ergonomics Society*, 58(8), 1217–1247. https://doi.org/10.1177/0018720816669646

Pigeon, J. (2021). *Guide pratique de la localisation vidéoludique en français canadien, précédé de l'état des lieux* (Master's dissertation). Université du Québec en Outaouais.

PlayOverwatch (2016). *Overwatch Animated Short | 'Alive'*. YouTube. https://youtu.be/U130wnpi-C0?t=293

PlayStation (2023). *Access Controller: A Customizable, Adaptive Controller Kit for PS5*. PlayStation Commercial Website. www.playstation.com/en-us/accessories/access-controller/

Prajzner, K. (2019). Narracja. In K. Prajzner (Ed.), *Wprowadzenie do groznawstwa* (pp. 15–36). Łódź: University of Lodz Press.

Radulovic, P. (2018, 29 June). *A 7-Year-Old Sims Mobile Game Is Being Pulled from Chinese App Stores*. Polygon. www.polygon.com/2018/6/29/17518170/the-sims-freeplay-removed-ios-android-china

Ramos, C. M. (2016). Testing audio narration: The emotional impact of language in audio description. *Perspectives: Studies in Translation Theory and Practice*, 24(4), 606–634. https://doi.org/10.1080/0907676x.2015.1120760

Ramos, M. (2015). The emotional experience of films: Does audio description make a difference? *The Translator*, 21(1), 68–94. https://doi.org/10.1080/13556509.2014.994853

Rauscher, A., Stein, D., & Thon, J.-N. (2021). *Comics and Videogames: From Hybrid Medialities to Transmedia Expansions*. New York: Routledge.

Remedy Entertainment (2019). *Control*. 505 Games.

Respawn Entertainment (2019). *Apex Legends*. Electronic Arts. www.ea.com/pl-pl/games/apex-legends/about/characters/bloodhound

Ribeiro, F., Florencio, D., Chou, P., & Zhang, Z. (2012). Auditory augmented reality: Object sonification for the visually impaired. IEEE 14th Int. *Workshop Multimedia Signal Process*, 319–324.

Roh, F. (2011). *Les Effets Des Erreurs De Traduction Dans La Localisation Des Jeux Vidéo (L'Exemple de The Elder Scrolls: IV Oblivion)*. (Master's dissertation) Geneva: University of Geneva. https://archive-ouverte.unige.ch/unige:17295

Rojo, A., Ramos, M., & Valenzuela, J. (2014). The emotional impact of translation: A heart rate study. *Journal of Pragmatics*, 71, 31–44. https://doi.org/10.1016/j.pragma.2014.07.006

Romero-Fresco, P. (2019). *Accessible Filmmaking: Integrating Translation and Accessibility into the Filmmaking Process*. London: Routledge. https://doi.org/10.4324/9780429053771

Ruskin, E. (2012). *AI-Driven Dynamic Dialog through Fuzzy Pattern Matching. Empower Your Writers!* GDC Vault. www.gdcvault.com/play/1015528/AI-driven-Dynamic-Dialog-through

Sajna, M. (2018). Cultural transfer in video games. *Linguistische Treffen in Wrocław*, 14, 175–186. https://doi.org/10.23817/lingtreff.14-15

Santa Monica Studio (2022). *God of War Ragnarök*. Sony Interactive Entertainment.

Sapkowski, A. (1990). *Wiedźmin* (The Witcher) [series] (Polish original). Various publishers.

Schafer, T. (2020). *Representing LGBT+ Characters in Games: Two Case Studies*. GDC Vault. www.gdcvault.com/play/1026629/Representing-LGBT-Characters-in-Games

Scherer, K. R. (2005). What are emotions? And how can they be measured? *Social Science Information*, 44(4), 695–729. https://doi.org/10.1177/0539018405058216

Shibayama, M. & Taniyama, H. (2012). Audio localization done right: Simultaneous scripting and recording. *Localization Summit 2012*. www.gdcvault.com/play/1015618/Audio-Localization-Done-Right-Simultaneous

Sony Interactive Entertainment (2023). *The Last of Us Part II – Accessibility*. PlayStation. www.playstation.com/en-us/games/the-last-of-us-part-ii/accessibility/

Square Enix (2023). *Final Fantasy XVI*. Square Enix.

St. Pierre, E. A. & Jackson, A. Y. (2014). Qualitative data analysis after coding. *Qualitative Inquiry*, 20(6), 715–719. https://doi.org/10.1177/1077800414532435

Sterczewski, P. (2012). Czytanie gry. O proceduralnej retoryce jako metodzie analizy ideologicznej gier komputerowych. *Teksty Drugie*, 6, 210–228. www.rcin.org.pl/dlibra/publication/65796

Sterling, J. S. (2009, 15 September). *Scribblenauts Getting a Full UK Localization*. Destructoid. www.destructoid.com/scribblenauts-getting-a-full-uk-localization/

Sue, J. (2018, 10 August). *Culture Clash: Why Arena of Valor Is Struggling in America*. GamesIndustry.biz. www.gamesindustry.biz/culture-clash-why-arena-of-valor-is-struggling-in-america

Suojanen, T., Koskinen, K., Tuominen, T. (2015), *User-Centered Translation*. London: Routledge.

Szarkowska, A. & Gerber-Morón, O. (2018). Viewers can keep up with fast subtitles: Evidence from eye movements. *PLOS (Public Library of Science) One*, 13(6) 1–30. https://doi.org/10.1371/journal.pone.0199331

Takatalo, J., Häkkinen, J., Kaistinen, J., & Nyman, G. (2010). Presence, involvement, and flow in digital games: Concepts and methods. In R. Bernhaupt (Ed.),

Evaluating User Experience in Games (pp. 23–46). Amsterdam: Springer. https://doi.org/10.1007/978-1-84882-963-3_3

Tales of Lumin (2023). *Baldur's Gate 3 Character Creation (All Races, Male & Female, Full Customization, All Options, More)*. YouTube. https://youtu.be/PXZVjESnsdg

Tal-Or, N. & Cohen, J. (2010). Understanding audience involvement: Conceptualizing and manipulating identification and transportation. *Poetics*, 38(4), 402–418. https://doi.org/10.1016/j.poetic.2010.05.004

Tango Gameworks (2022). *Ghostwire: Tokyo*. Bethesda Softworks.

TestronicLab (2023). *Localization QA*. Testronic. www.testroniclabs.com/localization-qa-2/

The Witcher (2015). *The Witcher 3: Wild Hunt – The Wolven Storm – Priscilla's Song (multilanguage)*. YouTube. www.youtube.com/watch?v=lMvAAfPs0UE

Tighe, D. (2023). *Bandai Namco Group: Gundam IP Sales FY2010 to FY2021*. Statista. www.statista.com/statistics/1304287/bandai-namco-mobile-suit-gundam-series-sales/

Ubisoft (2017). *Assassin's Creed Origins*. Ubisoft.

Ubisoft Montreal (2014). *Child of Light*. Ubisoft.

Unicef (2023). *Children's rights and online gaming: Industry toolkit on advancing diversity, equity and inclusion*. United Nations Children's Fund. www.unicef.org/reports/childrens-rights-and-online-gaming

USK (2023). *USK Altersfreigabe für Life Is Strange: True Colors*. Unterhaltungssoftware Selbstkontrolle. https://usk.de/en/usktitle/49168/

UsTwo (2023). *Desta: The Memories Between*. UsTwo.

Valve (2007). *Portal 2*. Valve.

VGE (2022). *All about Video Games: European Key Facts 2022*. Video Games Europe. www.videogameseurope.eu/publication/2022-all-about-video-games-european-key-facts/

Volition (2013). *Saints Row IV*. Deep Silver.

Wiemeyer, J., Nacke, L., Moser, C., & Floyd' Mueller, F. (2016). Player experience. In R. Dörner, S. Göbel, W. Effelsberg, & J. Wiemeyer (Eds.), *Serious Games: Foundations, Concepts and Practice* (pp. 243–271). Amsterdam: Springer. https://doi.org/10.1007/978-3-319-40612-1_9

Wijman, T. (2023). Newzoo's games market revenue estimates and forecasts by region and segment for 2023. https://newzoo.com/resources/blog/games-market-estimates-and-forecasts-2023

Witmer, B. G., & Singer, M. J. (1998). Measuring presence in virtual environments: A presence questionnaire. *Presence: Teleoperators and Virtual Environments*, 7(3), 225–240. https://doi.org/10.1162/105474698565686

Wu, Z. & Chen, Z. (2020). Localizing Chinese games for Southeast Asian markets: A multidimensional perspective. *The Journal of Internationalization and Localization*, 7(1–2), 49–68. https://doi.org/10.1075/jial.20003.wu

Xbox (2023). *Xbox Adaptive Controller.* Xbox Commercial Website. www .xbox.com/en-GB/accessories/controllers/xbox-adaptive-controller

Yuan, B. & Folmer, E. (2008). Blind hero: Enabling guitar hero for the visually impaired. *10th International ACM SIGACCESS Conference on Computers and Accessibility*, 169–176.

Zabalbeascoa, P. (2008). The nature of the audiovisual text and its parameters. In J. Díaz-Cintas (ed.), *The Didactics of Audiovisual Translation* (pp. 21–37). https://doi.org/10.1075/btl.77.05zab

Zanettin, F. (2008). *Comics in Translation*. Manchester: St. Jerome.

Zhang, X. (2013). Censorship and digital games localisation in China. *Censorial Forces at Play: Past and Present*, 57(2), 338–350. https://doi .org/10.7202/1013949ar

Zorrakin-Goikoetxea, I. (2023). Reflexión sobre el euskera como lengua minoritaria en videojuegos y estudio de recepción. *Qualderns*, 30, 139–151. https://doi.org/10.5565/rev/quaderns.106

Zulhusni, M. (2023). *Gaming in 2023: Asia's Influence on a Multi-billion Dollar Tech Industry*. TechHQ.com. https://techhq.com/2023/10/in-2023-what-the-west-probably-doesnt-know-about-eastern-gaming/

Acknowledgements

The authors wish to thank Prof. Kirsten Malmkjær, the Series Editor, as well as the two anonymous Reviewers, for their insightful feedback that considerably helped improve this Element.

Cambridge Elements ⁼

Translation and Interpreting

Elements in the Series